Ukulele Exercises

FOR

DUMMIES®

A Wiley Brand

Ukulele Exercises

FOR DUMMIES®

A Wiley Brand

by Brett McQueen

FOR DUMMIES®
A Wiley Brand

Ukulele Exercises For Dummies®

Published by:
John Wiley & Sons, Ltd
The Atrium, Southern Gate,
Chichester, West Sussex

www.wiley.com

This edition first published 2013

© 2013 John Wiley & Sons, Ltd, Chichester, West Sussex.

Registered office

John Wiley & Sons Ltd, The Atrium, Southern Gate, Chichester, West Sussex, PO19 8SQ, United Kingdom

For details of our global editorial offices, for customer services and for information about how to apply for permission to reuse the copyright material in this book please see our website at www.wiley.com.

The right of the author to be identified as the author of this work has been asserted in accordance with the Copyright, Designs and Patents Act 1988

For general information on our other products and services, please contact our Customer Care Department within the U.S. at 877-762-2974, outside the U.S. at (001) 317-572-3993, or fax 317-572-4002. For technical support, please visit www.wiley.com/techsupport.

For technical support, please visit www.wiley.com/techsupport.

A catalogue record for this book is available from the British Library.

ISBN 978-1-118-50685-1 (paperback) ISBN 978-1-118-50693-6 (ebk)

ISBN 978-1-118-50691-2 (ebk) ISBN 978-1-118-50694-3 (ebk)

Manufactured in the United States of America at Bind-Rite

10 9 8 7 6 5 4 3 2

Contents at a Glance

Table of Contents

Introduction

●●

Whether you've played ukulele for years or just started playing a couple of weeks ago, *Ukulele Exercises For Dummies* is a practice book for anyone who wants to become a better ukulele player. With hundreds of exercises and dozens of songs, you have a practice roadmap for improving your chops and becoming a more confident ukulele player. Through the exercises in this book, your fingers will come out stronger and more agile, and your mind will be sharpened and opened up to new and exciting ways of playing the ukulele through the different styles and techniques to which I introduce you.

One of the best parts of the ukulele is that it has such a relaxing, peaceful and joyful aura when played. Because the ukulele originates from Hawaii, some people say it carries the Hawaiian *Aloha Spirit*. It's hard to listen to someone play the ukulele and not crack a smile or grin from ear to ear (I dare you to try). In this way, this book isn't about rigorously practising an overwhelming amount of exercises; it's about equipping you to go from practice to playing those songs that carry the joyful spirit of the ukulele.

About This Book

Ukulele Exercises For Dummies isn't necessarily meant to be read from cover to cover like a normal book. The cool thing about this book (if I do say so myself) is that it's written so you can look over the table of contents and flip to the chapters that cover the techniques and aspects of playing the ukulele that interest you most. In fact, as you practise, you might choose several different exercises to practise at a time from multiple chapters.

At the same time the chapters of this book are organised and developed the way they are for good reasons. When learning about music, different concepts and ideas tend to compound and build on each other. This is only natural, and you should expect it. For example, in Part II 'Becoming a Better Strummer', Chapter 3 addresses a lot of foundational ways of thinking and approaching the strumming exercises that come in Chapter 4, 5 and 6. The goal through-out each part of the book is to develop and improve a particular aspect of your technique, so at times, there is a gradual but noticeable progression of growth throughout each chapter. In this way, if you do come across something that seems unfamiliar, flip a few pages back because it was most likely covered a little earlier. When later chapters pull on information taught in earlier chapters, I do my best to include a reference for you.

There are *a lot* of exercises in this book. The exciting thing about these exercises is that almost all of them are designed so you can come back to them even after you've 'mastered' the techniques. I say 'mastered' because I've been playing ukulele my entire life and I still use the exercises in this book in my practise sessions. These exercises will always assist as a way to challenge your fingers and improve your overall playing technique.

Because of the amount of exercises presented throughout this book, avoid tackling all of the exercises from a chapter in one sitting. It's best to take a couple of exercises from a chapter and spend time practising those for a day, week or month – however much time you need – before moving on. It's okay to mix and practise exercises from multiple chapters during your practice times, but if you do this, I recommend using a practice journal to write out the things you are practising to keep track of your progress. In Chapter 1, I discuss more about how to use a practice journal.

Overall, with this book, I want to help you unlock the parts to playing the ukulele that allow you to approach your playing more creatively and expressively, so you are able to go beyond the pages of this book and be more inspired as a musician and artist. To that end, along with the practice exercises, I include many songs in a variety of popular ukulele styles that you are able to learn and apply your skills.

Conventions Used in This Book

One of the most challenging aspects to learning and progressing at the ukulele can be sifting through the musical terms and lingo that gets thrown around. In this book, when I introduce an important, new term, I *italicise* the term and follow it with a definition. At the same time, there are a few common terms that show up over and over again that are worth going over since they can be confusing if you're a relatively new ukulele player.

For example, when I refer to your *fretting hand*, I'm talking about the hand that forms the chord positions and presses against the strings on the ukulele fretboard. If you're a right-handed player, your fretting hand is your left hand. If I refer to your *strumming hand* or *picking hand*, I'm talking about the hand that strums or plucks the strings. If you are a right-handed player, this is your right hand. For left-handed players, reverse hands.

All of the exercises in this book are written for a ukulele tuned in standard tuning: g-C-E-A. If I refer to the *top string* of the ukulele, I'm talking about the g-string, and if I refer to the *bottom string* of the ukulele, I'm talking about the A-string. Additionally, if I refer to the *1st string*, I'm talking about the A-string; the *2nd string* indicates the E-string; the *3rd string* indicates the C-string; and lastly, the *4th string* indicates the g-string.

In the context of strumming the ukulele, the terms *down* and *up* refer to the direction to strum across the strings. Strumming down requires you to strum starting from the top string to the bottom string. Strumming up requires you to strum starting from the bottom to the top string.

The terms *high* and *low* are often used in this book to refer to the pitch and positioning of a note on the ukulele fretboard. When I say a note is played *high* on the neck, I mean that the note is played on the fretboard of the ukulele closer to the sound hole. If a note is played *low* on the neck, it is played closer to the headstock. Thus, notes played higher up on the fretboard are higher in pitch, whereas notes played lower on the fretboard are lower in pitch.

There are two separate ways to indicate which fingers are used for an exercise. The numbers 1–4 are used to indicate the fingers in your fretting hand – often used for chord diagrams and in certain music notation. The number 1 indicates the index finger, number 2 the middle finger, number 3 the ring finger and number 4 the little finger (or pinky). When referring to your picking hand, four letters are used. The letter *p* indicates you pluck the string with your thumb, *i* indicates the index finger, *m* indicates the middle finger and *a* indicates the ring finger. This way of identifying fingers is unpacked more in the pages ahead.

Lastly, in an effort to present the exercises, this book makes use of ukulele tab and notation, chord and scale diagrams, and metronome markings, which are discussed and explained in more detail in Chapter 1.

What You're Not to Read

Each exercise in this book is created and presented with as much necessary information as possible, so if you wanted, you could play the exercises without having to read the surrounding text. At the same time, the explanations surrounding the exercises often give you helpful pointers and help you understand what you're playing on a deeper level, which gives you the ability to take the concepts behind the exercises and apply them to actual pieces of music.

More importantly, be sure to listen to the audio demonstrations that go along with the exercises. The audio is the biggest aspect to this book. These audio recordings provide a demonstration so you can get a really good, quick idea for how the exercise should sound and feel when you play it. Additionally, you can use these audio examples to play along with me. Notice that I play all of these audio examples to a metronome so you can get an idea of how to practise with a metronome too, if you have one. In Chapter 1, I talk more about using a metronome in your practice.

Foolish Assumptions

You don't have to have a lot of experience playing the ukulele in order to use this book. Throughout the book, I provide detailed explanations of the exercises to ensure you're up to speed with what's being presented. Still though, because this is a practice book, I try to spend less time talking and more time getting the ukulele in your hands with practice exercises. If you need information on things like learning basic chords, tuning the ukulele, or buying a ukulele, I highly recommend checking out *Ukulele For Dummies*.

The biggest assumption I do make is that you have a soprano, concert, or tenor ukulele that is tuned in standard tuning (g-C-E-A). Unfortunately, if you have a baritone ukulele tuned to D-G-B-E, or if you tune your ukulele to another tuning, you will be unable to follow along with the majority of the exercises presented in this book.

How This Book Is Organised

There are three main focuses to this book: strumming, fingerpicking and learning the ukulele fretboard. Within each of these focuses, there are many different techniques to learn and explore. Depending on the technique, each part of the book can look a little different in terms of what kind of exercises are used. Check out the following descriptions to get a bird's eye view of how this book is organised.

Part I: Getting Started with Ukulele Exercises

I get you up to speed on the things you need to know to get the most out of the exercises in this book. If you've been playing ukulele for awhile, chances are some of this information will be familiar for you. In Chapter 1, I recommend and explain the use of three different practice tools that make your practice sessions more productive. I also review how to read ukulele notation and tab, chord diagrams, scale diagrams and rhythm charts, which helps you easily follow along with the exercises in this book. In Chapter 2, you start warming up your fingers and hands with stretches, breathing exercises and strength-building exercises. You also pick up the ukulele and play through several practice exercises.

Part II: Becoming a Better Strummer

You strengthen your rhythm, timing and ability to find the right strumming pattern for any song. Because strumming is a form of rhythm, you learn how to count, feel and play to the beat. I teach you exercises that break down strumming into its simplest parts, and then, I show you how to add to these simple strumming patterns to make them more complex and interesting sounding for your listener. Throughout this part, you learn how to play more than a dozen songs in different styles. By the end of this part, you will be able to build your own strumming patterns that's right and fits for whatever song you're playing.

Part III: Becoming a Better Fingerpicker

There are a couple of different styles of fingerpicking on the ukulele. The first way is *rhythmic fingerpicking* (Chapter 8), where you fingerpick a repeating pattern that allows you to pick the chords and sing the melody of a song. The second way is *fingerstyle* (Chapter 9), where you take beautiful and intricate sounding classical guitar pieces and perform them on ukulele. The third way, which is another form of fingerstyle, is often referred to as *solo fingerpicking* (Chapter 10), where you fingerpick the melody of a song that is normally sung. Throughout this part, you practise a variety of picking exercises that improve the speed, flexibility and fluidity of your picking hand.

Part IV: Mastering the Ukulele Fretboard

To master the ukulele fretboard means to learn the notes of the fretboard and how you relate those notes with one another in meaningful ways to play songs. In this part, you learn how to build major and minor scales across the neck of the ukulele (Chapters 11 and 12), and then you see how those notes relate to one another by building chords in different positions across the ukulele fretboard (Chapter 13). This means you won't ever have to look at a chord diagram again. You also pick up some soloing techniques in musical styles like rock, blues and jazz (Chapter 14).

Part V: The Part of Tens

In case you're not familiar, in any *For Dummies* book, there is a special part of the book called the Part of Tens. This part breaks away from the exercises in the rest of the book to give you some extra, free-of-charge tips about improving your practice sessions (Chapter 15) and learning about how to take those steps to taking your ukulele skills and performing for an audience (Chapter 16). Both of these chapters include ten quick tips that you can apply to your ukulele playing today.

Accessing the Audio Tracks

Ukulele Exercises For Dummies comes with 256 audio tracks – each one an essential aid to mastering the songs, techniques and exercises that I cover in the book. If you've purchased the paper or e-book version of *Ukulele Exercises For Dummies*, just go to www.dummies. com/go/ukuleleexercises to access and download these tracks. (If you don't have internet access, call 877-762-2974 within the U.S. or 317-572-3993 outside the U.S.) Each exercise in the book which ties into an audio track has the track number above it in a black box, so you'll always be able to match what you see on the page to what you're hearing.

Icons Used in This Book

In the left-hand margins of this book, you'll find the following icons:

This icon reminds you of important information that is essential to playing the ukulele. This is the stuff you never want to forget.

Every now and then I go a little deeper in my explanations of certain musical terms, techniques, or ideas. This icon indicates interesting information that is a bit more technical. Not essential, but you might find it interesting.

These quick pointers help make the exercises and songs easier to play or understand.

I use this icon to caution you of anything that could cause discomfort, pain or injury to you or your ukulele.

Where to Go from Here

Flip right over to Chapter 1 if you need a refresher on some of the basics. To get your hands warmed up and ready to practise, start at Chapter 2 for some stretches and exercises. If you are a relatively new ukulele player, after going over Chapter 1 and 2, I recommend starting at Part II 'Becoming a Better Strummer' as this will get you playing some of the 'staple' ukulele songs right away. If you've been playing ukulele for awhile, or if you already have a pretty specific practice routine, skip around through the book to pick and choose exercises you'd like to add to your routine to improve different aspects of your technique.

Part I

Getting Started with Ukulele Exercises

getting started with

Ukulele Exercises

Go to www.dummies.com/go/ukuleleexercises to listen to audio tracks.

In this part . . .

- ✔ Learn three different practice tools to make your practice sessions more productive.

- ✔ Review ukulele tablature and the different sorts of diagram you'll come across.

- ✔ Pick up tips on how to warm up for practice.

- ✔ Pick up your uke and get started on practice.

- ✔ Go to www.dummies.com/go/ukuleleexercises to listen to audio tracks accompanying this book.

Chapter 1

Preparing to Practise

In This Chapter

▶ Looking at three essential practice tools

▶ Brushing up on ukulele tab and notation

Many exciting exercises lie ahead in the coming chapters. With your hard work and practice, you're going to see amazing improvements in your ukulele playing, but before picking up your ukulele, take a moment to cover some essentials. In this chapter, you discover three helpful practice tools that enable you to get the most out of the exercises in this book, and you review how to read ukulele tab and notation, which allows you to easily follow along with the exercises I present in this book.

Equipping Yourself with the Right Practice Tools

While the following tools aren't necessary or required to enjoy the exercises in the pages ahead, they can make your practice times more productive and effective.

Tuning up with a chromatic tuner

It's always a good idea to tune up your ukulele every time you practise. Through playing, and through small changes in temperature and humidity, the strings of the ukulele go out of tune. An in-tune ukulele is always more inspiring to play and listen to than one that is out of tune.

In standard ukulele tuning, from the top to bottom string, a ukulele is tuned to a G note above middle C on the piano, middle C, E above middle C, and A above middle C. In this way, a ukulele is tuned: g-C-E-A (the lower case 'g' represents the high g-string).

The ukulele can be tuned in a variety of different ways, but the exercises in this book are created for ukuleles tuned to standard tuning. To learn more about other ukulele tunings, be sure to check out *Ukulele For Dummies* by Alistair Wood.

Tuning your ukulele is easy if you have a piano nearby, but more often than not, this isn't the case. The easiest and most accurate way to tune your ukulele is to use a *chromatic tuner*. A chromatic tuner is a small, inexpensive, portable electronic device that listens to each string you pluck on the ukulele and tells you whether that string needs to be tuned higher or lower in pitch. I strongly recommend you purchase a chromatic tuner at your local music store, or if you have a smartphone, purchase and download a chromatic tuner app to your device.

Keeping time with a metronome

A metronome is a small device that helps strengthen your sense of timing (musically referred to as *tempo*) by producing a short, consistent 'click' sound. By lining up your ukulele playing with the 'click' of a metronome, you improve your timing and rhythm, which creates a more pleasing sounding performance for your listener. You can buy a metronome at any music store or you can purchase a metronome app for your smartphone. Additionally, some chromatic tuners are combined with a metronome for just a little bit more money.

Tempo is measured in *beats per minute* (BPM). Typically, a slow tempo is considered anywhere around 40 to 60 BPM and a fast tempo is considered 120 BPM or higher. For some of the exercises and songs in this book, I notate a suggested tempo at the beginning of the figure. In music notation, tempo is often indicated with a quarter note and a number, as shown in the following figure.

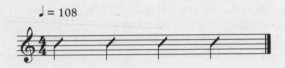

These suggested tempos throughout the book should be seen as a goal. If you set your metronome at the suggested tempo and you are unable to play the song or exercise that fast, slow down the tempo to a speed that allows you to play without mistakes. Then, gradually increase the speed in small increments to play at the suggested tempo.

While practising, don't use a metronome all the time. Sometimes the pressure of keeping time with a metronome can create tension in your playing, which works against you. First, spend time practising the exercises and songs in this book without a metronome, and then, to tighten up your timing and rhythm, add in the use of the metronome.

Tracking your progress with a practice journal

Truthfully, this book contains a lot of exercises. To get the most out of your practice sessions, and to become a better ukulele player, it's important you're practising in a focused way. This means it's best to select a few exercises to work on at a time from different sections of this book. The exercises aren't meant to be tackled all at once.

I highly recommend using a practice journal to focus your practice sessions, and to prevent yourself from getting overwhelmed. A pen and a notebook will do the trick, or you can create an updatable text file on your personal computer.

Here are a couple of different ways to use a practice journal:

✔ **Create a practice plan for the week.** For example, one day you might work on a couple of major scale patterns from Chapter 11, then, the next day, select a few rhythmic fingerpicking patterns to learn from Chapter 8, and then later on, to cap it off, practise a handful of strumming patterns from Chapter 4. You might mix these things up on the same day, but whatever you decide, write it out, so you know exactly what you're practising throughout the week.

✔ **Identify successes and current challenges.** After you practise, take a minute to list out your successes. For example, you might note in your journal, 'Able to successfully fingerpick Carcassi's 'Andantino' from Chapter 9 at a moderate tempo.' In addition, write out challenges, like, 'Need to work on fretting the notes in measures 7 and 8 of Carcassi's 'Andantino' in Chapter 9.' By writing these successes and challenges out, you can be encouraged in your practice and identify exactly what you need to work on for the next practice session.

✔ **Write out measurable goals.** Think about where you want to be in a week, a month, six months, or a year. You might write out things like, 'I want to learn and memorise all C major scale positions from Chapter 11 in two weeks,' or, 'I want to be able to play Tárrega's 'Étude in E minor' from Chapter 9 at 92 BPM in a month.' The more specific you can be in your goals the more it can inform you about how to structure your practice times and help focus you in practising the things that help you reach your goal.

Throughout the following chapters, I give you some more recommendations for how to use your practice journal. Give it a try and see how it works for you.

Reviewing Ukulele Notation

Depending on the concepts and techniques I'm teaching you, the exercises in this book are presented in a few different ways. You don't need to be a pro at reading music in order to use the exercises and songs in this book, but it is helpful to review some of the basics.

Deciphering tablature

Tablature, often just called *tab*, is a simplified form of musical notation for the ukulele. Unlike regular music notation, tab shows exactly where to play the notes of an exercise or song across the ukulele's fretboard.

In the most basic way, in ukulele tab, there are four lines, with each line representing a different string of the ukulele, as shown in the following figure.

Tab is drawn from the perspective as if you are holding the ukulele in playing position and looking over the neck of the ukulele down at the strings. In this way, the top line of the ukulele tab represents the bottom or 1st string of the ukulele, and the bottom line of the ukulele tab represents the top or 4th string of the ukulele.

The numbers on each line represent a fret number. For example, in the previous figure, the number 3 on the top line means you press down on the 3rd fret of the 1st string of the ukulele, or more accurately, in between the space between the 2nd and 3rd fret on the bottom string. Likewise, the number 5 on the third line from the top means you press down on the 5th fret of the 3rd string. If you see a number 0, that you means you pluck the open string, without touching the string with your fretting hand.

Tab is commonly used to represent single-note melody lines or fingerpicking patterns (such as those in Part III of this book), but tab can also be used to represent chords. If the numbers line up vertically across multiple strings, that means you fret and sound the notes across those strings all at once.

Using tab to represent music is advantageous because of how easy it is to read the notes, but the downside to using tab is that often times tablature doesn't express note durations, meaning, it can be hard to tell how long to hold certain notes just from a piece of tab. For this reason, and for your benefit, the tab in almost all of the exercises in this book is presented in combination with actual music notation.

Understanding chord diagrams

A *chord diagram* is a representation of a chord's finger position on the neck of the ukulele. The chord diagram should be seen and read as if you were holding the ukulele up vertically in front of you and looking directly at the fretboard.

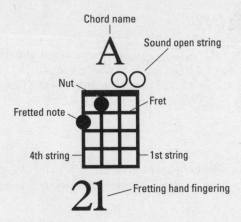

The capital letter at the top of the diagram tells you the name of the chord. In the figure above, the letter 'A' indicates that this is an A major chord. Additional letters and numbers might follow the letter to indicate other chord qualities (minor, dominant seventh, major seventh, etc.).

The vertical lines represent each of the four strings of the ukulele. The horizontal lines represent frets. The thick black horizontal line at the top of the diagram is representative of the nut of the ukulele. The black dots represent the notes that are fretted on the ukulele.

The numbers at the bottom of the chord diagram indicate which finger you should use to fret the note on the string. The index finger is represented by the number '1', middle finger by the number '2', ring finger by the number '3', and the little finger by the number '4'.

In some cases, chord diagrams indicate chords played at higher positions on the fretboard. For example, at the right of the E7 chord in the following figure, the number and letters *4fr* indicate the starting notes of the chord are played at the 4th fret. The curved line arching over the three notes on the 4th fret indicate a *barre*; meaning, at the 4th fret, you fret the notes by laying a finger over the strings (usually the index finger). The Bb and F# chords show other ways a barre shows up in a ukulele chord, although you might decide to use your index finger to barre all four strings for these chords too.

Chord diagrams give you a suggestion for the chord's fingering. You might find alternate fingerings that make more sense and work better than others in the context of certain chord progressions and songs.

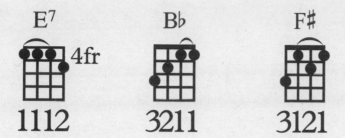

Comprehending neck diagrams

A *neck diagram* is a visual representation of notes across the ukulele fretboard. In this book, I use neck diagrams to demonstrate different scale positions and note names across the fretboard. Neck diagrams are like tab in that the top line of the neck diagram represents the bottom or 1st string of the ukulele, and the bottom line of the diagram represents the top or 4th string of the ukulele. The perspective is as if you are holding the ukulele in playing position and looking over the neck of the ukulele down at the fretboard.

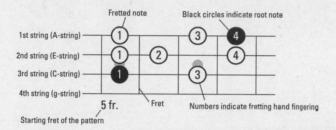

Most of the time, neck diagrams are used to show a scale's position on the ukulele fretboard. At the bottom of the diagram, the number and letters *5fr* indicate that the starting note of the scale position starts on the 5th fret.

Each circle represents a note you fret with a finger on the fretboard. Filled in circles represent the root note of a scale. For example, the previous figure shows an F major scale pattern on the bottom three strings of the ukulele. The black dot on the 5th fret of the 3rd string and the 8th fret of the 1st string represents an 'F' note, which is the root note of an F major scale.

The numbers in the circles indicate which finger to use to fret the note. The index finger is represented by the number '1', middle finger by the number '2', ring finger by the number '3', and the little finger by the number '4'. In some examples, where I demonstrate the name of the notes across the fretboard, the name of the note is shown in the circle rather than the fingering.

Reading rhythm charts

A *rhythm chart* is written on a normal music staff, but rather than indicating actual notes, the chart indicates the rhythm of a strumming pattern. The chord diagram above the music indicates which chord you strum.

In this figure, the rhythm chart is written in 4/4 time signature; meaning, there are four beats per measure. *Rhythm slashes* or black lines going through the music staff represent quarter notes and eighth notes (more on those in Part II).

The numbers and letters below the chart are what you want to concern yourself most with. The numbers help you count out loud the strumming pattern. The letters 'd' and 'u' indicate which direction to strum across the strings: down or up.

Chapter 2

Warming Up for Practice

. . . .

In This Chapter

▶ Finding the best way to hold the ukulele

▶ Learning a variety of warm up exercises and stretches

. . . .

Playing the ukulele can be a lot like running a race. To run the best you can, you have to ensure your body is stretched out and warmed up in advance. Like playing the ukulele, you prevent a lot of soreness and fatigue during your practice if you take a few minutes to warm up. Properly warming up also has additional benefits, adding speed, fluidity and smoothness to your ukulele playing.

In this chapter, you look at a few key stretches and exercises that help loosen, relax and strengthen your fingers and hands to more effortlessly play the ukulele. Then, you take a quick look at holding the ukulele to find the most comfortable playing posture. Lastly, you pick up your ukulele as I show you a variety of simple warm-up exercises. These exercises help get your fingers ready for the exercises and songs in the pages to come.

Limbering Up Your Body to Play Ukulele

Don't pick up the ukulele just yet. First, use the following stretches and exercises to warm up your fingers, hands, wrist and body to minimise fatigue and to give yourself more energy to play and practise for longer periods of time.

Don't overdo these stretches and exercises or you might experience cramping and soreness. From each section, just choose a couple rather than trying to tackle them all at once.

Loosening up with stretches

For the most part, playing the ukulele uses your hands, fingers and wrists. To start waking up these areas of the body, stretch each of your hands by alternating between making a fist and opening up your fingers as far as possible. By moving your hand in this basic way, you get the blood flowing and start to loosen up your hand.

After you do that, use the following stretches to stretch your hand and wrist:

✔ **Rotating Hand Stretch:** Hold your hand in a loose fist and from your wrist slowly rotate clockwise and counter-clockwise. Likewise, open up your hand so your fingers are relaxed and repeat the rotating motion from the wrist. For each stretch, rotate in each direction a few times.

✔ **'Halt!' Stretch:** Fully extend your arm as if you were raising your hand to tell someone to stop or halt. While keeping this 'Stop' position in your hand, with a straight arm and locked elbow, take your other hand and pull the targeted hand back towards your body. Hold for five seconds and release.

✔ **Inverted 'Halt!' Stretch:** Similar to the last stretch, from the 'Stop' hand position, let your hand go limp. Then, point your fingers down to the ground, while keeping a straight arm and locked elbow. Take your other hand and pull back the targeted hand towards the ground and towards your body. Hold for five seconds and release.

In addition to stretching your fingers, hands and wrist, it's a good idea to take a minute to stretch out the rest of your body. In a standing position, extend your arms into the air and reach as high as you can. You should feel the muscles in your arms, shoulders and back stretch. Lastly, in a relaxed standing position, with your arms to your side, tilt your head to the left, right, forwards and backwards to stretch out your neck. These simple stretches loosen up your neck and shoulders, which can benefit your overall playing posture.

Relaxing with breathing exercises

Breathing exercises are beneficial in a few ways. For one, they having a relaxing effect throughout your body and muscles, which is perfect for combatting tension. Through breathing exercises, you increase the amount of oxygen your body receives, which lowers your heart rate, increases mental alertness, decreases stress and overall, gives you more energy. Try out a couple of these breathing exercises before you pick up and play your ukulele.

✔ **Relaxing Breath Exercise:** While sitting up or lying down, first, breath out all the air completely from your lungs. Then, inhale for five seconds. In that period, try to evenly inhale as much air as possible and as deeply as possible. Next, hold your breath for another five seconds. Lastly, evenly exhale all of the air from your lungs for five seconds. Repeat the exercise a couple times.

✔ **Hissing Breath Exercise:** This exercise is popular among singers because it helps control your breathing while producing a relaxing effect. In a sitting or lying position, first, breath out all the air from your lungs. Then, take a big, deep breath. For 15–20 seconds, exhale the air from your lungs while producing a 'hissing' sound like a snake. Try to make the hissing sound as light and as even as possible as to not let all the air out at once. Repeat the exercise again. As you get better, try to extend the length of your exhale up to as high as a minute.

✔ **Stimulating Breath Exercise:** Use this exercise to increase energy and raise alertness. While sitting up, with your mouth closed in a relaxed position, inhale and exhale as quickly as possible through your nose for no longer than 10–15 seconds. If you do it quickly, the exercise should produce a noisy breathing sound.

Perform these breathing exercises in small, short amounts at first to prevent lightheadedness, dizziness, or hyperventilation.

Strengthening your hands with exercises

Whether you're trying to fret a chord or fingerpick a pattern on the ukulele, you need a certain degree of strength and endurance to execute those aspects of playing in a clean and effortless way. The following exercises help strengthen your fingers, hands and wrist.

✔ **Praying Hands Exercise:** While sitting or standing, take the palms of both hands and put them together as if you are praying. The tips of the fingers from each hand should touch the tips of the fingers from the other hand. Separate your palms slightly while keeping the fingers of each hand touching the fingers of the other hand. Then, push your fingers from each hand against each other equally to create pressure. Hold this pressure for 5–10 seconds. Repeat the exercise twice.

- ✔ **Squeezing Exercise:** Take a tennis ball or bean bag in either hand. Squeeze the tennis ball with a moderately high amount of pressure for 5–10 seconds. Release the pressure for five seconds. Repeat 5–10 times.

- ✔ **Edge of the Table Exercise:** While sitting down at a table, lay your fingers at the edge of the table while keeping your fingers and hand straight but reasonably relaxed. Push down against the table with your fingers to create pressure throughout your hand. Hold this positions for 5–10 seconds. Then, relax for five seconds. Repeat a few times.

Performing these exercises will probably cause soreness throughout your hand, in the same way that your legs would feel sore after a run. Only perform these exercises in small amounts before a practice session, and if you experience any pain, be sure to stop immediately and take a break.

Brushing Up on Perfect Playing Posture

Before I show you some warm-up exercises on the ukulele, take a moment to evaluate your playing posture. How you hold the ukulele depends a lot on your body size and the size of your ukulele. It also depends on whether you're sitting down or standing up.

For sitting down and playing the ukulele, cradle the body of the ukulele with the arm of your strumming hand, while the part of your forearm closest to the elbow applies a little pressure to the top of the ukulele, so it is held snug against your body. Then support the neck of the ukulele in the crevice of your fretting hand where your thumb meets the index finger.

When standing up, it's a good idea to invest in a ukulele strap to provide support for holding the ukulele. Even while sitting down, you might want to use a strap for that extra support. Professional ukulele players like Jake Shimabukuro and James Hill are known for using a ukulele strap while they stand up to perform.

Your overall playing posture should allow you to sit or stand up straight in a relaxed way. Avoid hunching over the ukulele. The key is to find a comfortable and relaxed playing position that allows the ukulele to be as stable as possible. As you play the ukulele, it's normal for it to move around a little bit within your hands as you change chords and strum. In this way, don't try to grip the ukulele very tightly – just enough to provide support.

Looking at Some Warm-Up Exercises on the Ukulele

It's time to pick up the ukulele and warm up your fingers with a couple of exercises. The first group of exercises focuses on single-note exercises, which get your fingers ready to move and change between different notes across the fretboard. The second group of exercises focuses on prepping your fingers for changing between various chords.

Practising single-note exercises

The following single-note exercises stretch and warm up the fingers in your fretting hand. In these exercises, you pluck one note at a time on an individual string. Use your thumb to pluck each note of the exercise.

This first exercise is an ascending and descending sequence that uses the index, middle, ring and little fingers of your fretting hand. Assign your index finger to fret the notes that fall on the 1st fret, middle finger to the 2nd fret, ring finger to the 3rd fret and little finger to the 4th fret. At the end of the exercise, repeat the exercise one fret higher.

Track 1

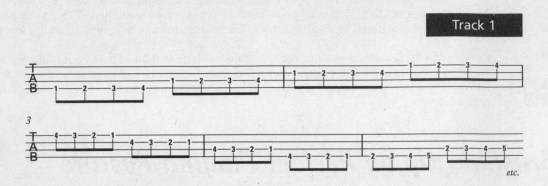

This next exercise is like the first in that you use your index, middle, ring and little fingers to pluck consecutive notes on the same string, but for this exercise move the position up a fret as you change strings.

Track 2

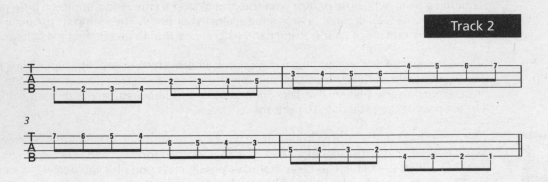

Change it up a little bit for this next exercise. This time ascend and descend each string with just two fingers. Assign your index finger to fret the notes that fall on the 1st fret, middle finger to the 2nd fret, ring finger to the 3rd fret and little finger to the 4th fret.

Track 3

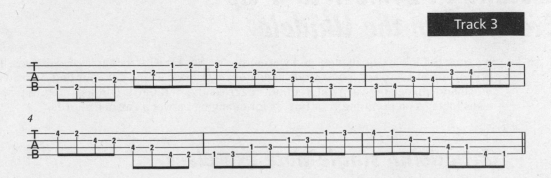

For this next exercise, stretch your fingers a little bit more. Assign your index finger to fret the notes that fall on the 1st fret, ring finger to the 3rd fret and little finger to the 5th fret. After you practise it that way, substitute your ring finger with your middle finger to play the notes that fall on the 3rd fret.

Track 4

This last exercise is like the previous one in that there is a gap between each note in the ascending and descending sequence of notes; however, in this exercise, move up a fret each time you change strings.

Track 5

Practising chord exercises

The following warm-up exercises get your fingers used to switching between a variety of different common chords. By cycling through these chord progressions, you improve your ability to change chords more quickly and improve the strength and dexterity in your fretting hand. For each exercise, take time to look at the chord diagrams and practise each chord individually. Strum each chord four times before changing to the next chord.

This first exercise makes use of some of the most common ukulele chords. A lot of the exercises in this book use these chords or variations on these chords.

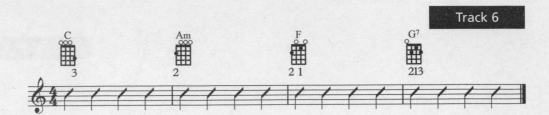

Think about setting up each chord change. For example, in the previous figure, while you're fretting the C chord with your ring finger on the 3rd fret of the bottom string, hover your middle finger over the 2nd fret of the top string to prepare for the Am chord.

The next chord progression introduces a couple more common chords.

The following exercise requires you to move your fingers around a little bit more. The trickiest chord is the D7 chord because you're required to use your index finger to barre or hold down the strings at the 2nd fret. This chord requires more strength, so take your time to ensure that every note of the chord rings out clearly.

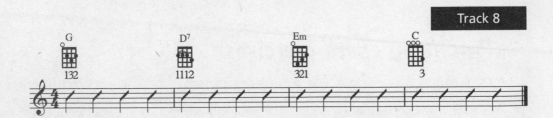

There are a couple more barre chords in this next exercise. For the Bm7 and C#m7 chords, use your index finger to barre all the strings. Ensure your thumb is firmly planted on the neck of the ukulele to provide support and leverage.

The toughest chord in the next exercise is the B♭ chord. You're required to perform a half barre with your index finger on the 1st fret of the bottom two strings. If you're not able to bend your finger in this way, you might use your index finger to barre all four strings at the 1st fret.

Track 10

Part II
Becoming a Better Strummer

*Five Great Ways to Make Strumming
Patterns More Interesting*

- **Create your own strumming pattern.** Changing around the order of down and up strums within the count. Try mixing quarter-note strums on the second and fourth beats with eighth-note strums on the first and third beats.

- **Use syncopation.** Syncopation comes in three different flavours, and gives your playing more variation – and even a jazzy feel – by changing the stress on beats. Choose from missed beat, suspended and off-beat syncopation.

- **Rearrange up strums to create different feels.** When you emphasise the offbeat in your strumming, you're able to create some really interesting rhythms, so challenge your internal timing clock and feel the offbeat.

- **Experiment with 3/4 time.** Use versatile 3/4 strumming patterns, which you can to give your playing a waltzy mood.

- **Take strumming to a new level.** Get more advanced with 6/8 time strumming patterns, using six beats per measure to give your playing a rhythmic, driving feel.

Go to www.dummies.com/go/ukuleleexercises to listen to audio tracks.

In this part . . .

- ✔ Learn how to strengthen your rhythm and timing.
- ✔ Discover how to build the right strumming pattern for any song.
- ✔ Develop a range of strumming patterns suited to different musical styles.
- ✔ Handle chord changes with ease.
- ✔ Refine your playing with advanced strumming techniques.
- ✔ Go to www.dummies.com/go/ukuleleexercises to hear 'Oh! Susanna' (Track 68, described in Chapter 5) played on the uke.

Chapter 3

Foundations for Strumming

- -

In This Chapter

▶ Refining strumming technique

▶ Finding the right strumming pattern for any song

▶ Singing and playing ukulele at the same time

- -

The ukulele is a relatively small instrument, so, naturally, it has a smaller sound when compared with an instrument like the guitar. You might think this is a bad thing, but when it comes to strumming, the ukulele's bright, 'chimey' tone makes it a strong rhythmic force perfect for singing along to with your friends (yes, even on the beach!) or jamming out with other ukulele players and instruments.

Every song you strum on the ukulele has a particular way or feel about it. The things that make a song a *song* include how you strum the strings of the ukulele, what strumming pattern you use, the speed at which you play, how consistently you maintain that speed, and your ability to play and change chords smoothly – not to mention actually singing the song. The ability to execute all of these skills at the same time takes a song from just being okay to being really great.

This may seem like a lot to juggle, and it kind of is! Not to fret though. The strumming exercises in this part of the book help you to home in on and develop all these skills. Before we crack the lid on those, however, this business of strumming actually becomes a whole lot easier if we lay some important groundwork.

In this chapter, I help you further develop and refine your strumming technique. I look at a few techniques and how each pulls a different tone out of the ukulele. Different songs and contexts call for different ways of strumming the ukulele, so you need to be ready! Second, I explore a way of thinking about strumming that allows you to figure out the right strumming pattern for any song. In addition, you find out how to become more proficient at singing and playing the ukulele at the same time.

Working Out Your Strumming Technique

How you strum the ukulele affects your ability to produce a tone from the ukulele that doesn't make you or your audience cringe with pain. A good tone from the ukulele is one that is consistent, even and balanced-sounding.

Many people find that using your dominant hand to strum is the most natural thing to do. However, there are always exceptions. For example, although I am a dominant left-hander, I find it more natural to use my left hand on the fretboard to play chords and my right hand to strum the strings. In this way, although I'm a lefty, I technically play ukulele right-handed. If you're just starting out on ukulele, you have to decide which route you want to take. When it comes to actual strumming technique, you can strum the ukulele in a few different ways.

Each way has its advantages and disadvantages, but because people have different body sizes and shapes, it's likely one of these ways will feel more natural to you over another. Take some time trying out each of these techniques.

Whatever you do, don't use a nylon guitar pick to strum the ukulele. A nylon pick produces a 'clicky' tone that is harsh and brittle. While a felt or soft pick is a better option, using only your fingers allows you to pull a more desirable and expressive tone from the ukulele. Plus, your fingers are crucial for more advanced strumming techniques.

Choosing the right strumming technique

As you try each of the techniques outlined in the following sections, notice how each pulls a different tone and sound out of the ukulele. For example, strumming with the ball of your thumb produces a softer, rounder tone, while strumming with the nail side of your index finger produces a brighter, more lively tone.

In all of this, there isn't a hard and fast, right or wrong way to strum the ukulele. Here I give you the most common ways of strumming the ukulele. How you strum the ukulele will largely depend on the tone you want to pull out of the ukulele and the type of song you are playing. These different strumming techniques work better in some applications over others. This is why it's important to take time, experiment, and practise with each of these techniques.

The main goal in all of this is to be able to strum the ukulele in a way that produces a consistent, even and balanced sound. This means your down strums and up strums should be nearly the same volume and intensity. Imagine your fingers gliding over the strings in one quick, relaxed motion. You don't need to dig into the strings to create sound. Just a little bit of a contact will produce a beautiful sound.

If you had to just learn one strumming technique really well, either the index finger technique or the four-finger strumming technique works ninety-nine per cent of the time for most songs.

Strumming with your index finger

To strum with your index finger, position your hand and fingers as if you're counting the number 'one' so the index finger is extended and the other fingers are curled into your hand in a very relaxed, limp sort of way. Use the nail side of your index finger for down strokes, and use the flesh side of your index finger for up strokes. Remember to strum with a loose hand and wrist. The advantages and disadvantages are:

Advantages

When you strum with your index finger, the motion for the strum comes from your wrist more than from your finger. Because of this, using your index finger allows you to strum more quickly and fluidly. Using your index finger can also create a brighter tone from the ukulele than you would get from using your thumb.

Disadvantages

The trick with using your index finger to strum is to keep your index finger very relaxed. Your wrist and the rest of your fingers, while curled into your hand, need to be just as relaxed too. It may be difficult to get your index finger relaxed enough so it isn't digging into the strings in a harsh way or even getting caught in between the strings.

Strumming with your thumb

When strumming the ukulele with your thumb, use the flesh side of your thumb for down strums, and use the side of your thumb, or the nail side of your thumb for up strums. Alternatively, you might add in the use of the previous strumming technique by using the flesh side of your thumb for down strums and the flesh side of the index finger for up strums. This creates an even more delicate, soft sound.

Advantages

With this technique, the flesh on the ball of your thumb has the ability to glide over the strings evenly and create a warm, soft tone from the ukulele. This is desirable for tender songs like lullabies.

Disadvantages

If you use your thumb to strum, it's tempting to leave your hand and wrist in one position and only pivot your thumb up and down from the joint connecting your thumb to your hand for your strumming movement. Unfortunately, this really limits your strumming because you restrict the movement of your entire strumming hand. Strumming is all about the loose and relaxed wrist, so if you wish to use your thumb to strum, remember to stay relaxed.

If you strum with your thumb, you might also be tempted to use your remaining four fingers to hold the body of the ukulele around the bottom side for support. Instead, it's better to practise good posture for holding the ukulele (see Chapter 2), since gripping the side of the ukulele with your fingers further prohibits the movement of your strumming hand.

Strumming with four fingers

For this strumming technique, extend your dominant strumming hand and give a thumbs up. Your index, middle, ring, and little finger should be folded back into the palm of your hand, so the tips of your fingers are pointing towards your elbow. Be sure to relax your hand so you aren't clenching any fingers. There should be space in your hand to hold a golf club.

With that position in place, use the nail side of your index, middle, and ring fingers for down strums. Use the side or nail side of your thumb for up strums. You might even find it more natural to use the flesh side of your index, middle and ring fingers for up strums. Bend your little finger back slightly if it is getting in the way.

For another variation on this technique, be sure to refer to *Ukulele For Dummies, 1st Edition*.

Advantages

At first, this way of strumming might seem a little bit peculiar, but there are many advantages, since you're using more fingers to strum. This is my favourite way to strum the ukulele. Here's why:

- ✔ Because you're making contact to the strings with three fingers, the tone produced can be richer and fuller sounding.

- ✔ Use this to your advantage and more easily control how soft or loud you are playing.

- ✔ Assuming you're strumming from a loose, relaxed hand and wrist, this technique allows you to easily play fast or slow strumming patterns.

- ✔ Using more fingers allows you to more easily transition into more advanced strumming techniques like rolling strums.

Discovering the strumming 'sweet spot'

Where you strum the ukulele is just as important as how you strum the ukulele. Every ukulele has a strumming *sweet spot*. Since each ukulele is different, this spot will be in a different place.

If you strum the ukulele across the neck, away from the sound hole, and closer towards your fretting hand – that is, you strum around the 5th to 10th fret – the sound produced will be warm and smooth, but you might notice there is a lack of definition between each string, to the point where it almost sounds muddy. On the flip side, if you strum across the strings right next to the bridge of the ukulele, you'll notice the sound is quite sharp and bright.

When you've hit the sweet spot, you get the most *balanced* tone from the ukulele, meaning that the tone from the ukulele isn't too muddy or too bright – it's just right. The sweet spot on most ukuleles is around where the neck or fretboard meets the body of the ukulele. For a larger sized ukulele, like a tenor or baritone, the sweet spot is usually closer to the sound hole.

Disadvantages

As with any of the other techniques, if you're not careful to relax your hand and strum from a loose wrist, this technique can come across as rigid and uncomfortable.

Getting Acquainted With the Golden Rules of Strumming

Setting some ground rules can help focus you on being able to find the right strumming pattern for *any* song. However, I have to be honest with you. As a musician and artist, I love breaking the rules. Maybe you're like me. This is why I like the ukulele so much. It's an instrument for rule-breakers. Just look at artists like James Hill, Jake Shimabukuro, the Ukulele Orchestra of Great Britain, and many others. These are folks who are constantly reinventing what can and can't be done with the ukulele.

Creating something different and interesting is always fun. However, in being creative, the limitations that come with certain guidelines and rules can actually help focus us on what we're creating. It goes without saying that, in order to break the rules well, you have to know what they are.

These rules for strumming are important for two main reasons:

✔ They help point to areas you can always be improving, even after you've attained more advanced levels of playing.

✔ Becoming a better ukulele player becomes less overwhelming and more manageable since you can always incorporate these rules into your practice and playing.

All of the strumming exercises in this book are centered around the three following rules. If you know these like the back of your hand, you're way beyond the vast majority of ukulele players.

Rule #1: Strumming is consistent

Strumming is a form of rhythm. Rhythm is the underlying force that carries a song's melody and harmony – that is, the vocal line and chords.

Musical rhythm is created through repeated patterns of variation between silence and strong and weak sounds of differing lengths.

In the case of strumming, how you arrange the order of down strums and up strums, how hard or soft you emphasise certain strums, how long you hold certain strums, and your ability to repeat this arrangement consistently, creates rhythm through a *strumming pattern*.

The most important part in all of this is that in order for rhythm to be effective it must be *consistent*. When it comes to strumming a pattern, you should avoid varying between fast and slow. At its best, strumming is performed at a consistent, steady speed or *tempo*. How loud or soft your playing is might change throughout a song, but the tempo does not.

Consistency is important in music because it creates a sense of predictability in a song. This sort of predictability gives the listener a feeling they can engage and be apart of what is happening in the song, such as through singing along.

Strumming isn't about being fancy. You can play the most complicated strumming pattern, but if it isn't executed smoothly and with consistent timing, you've completely defeated the purpose of strumming. Strumming is the backbone of a song and your listener is counting on you to create a strong, consistent foundation for the song.

If you want to improve your strumming by light-years, focus on making your strumming more consistent in tempo and tone. A great way to do this is to practise with a metronome. Practising with a metronome helps build and strengthen your internal tempo clock. In the strumming exercises that follow this chapter, I suggest tempos, so you can use a metronome as you practise.

Rule #2: Strumming is relaxed

There is good tension, and then there is bad tension. In order to play the ukulele, you need a certain amount of tension and strength, as when you're fretting chords and strumming the strings. However, when tension hampers your ability to perform these functions smoothly, it's bad.

Bad tension makes your playing rigid, stiff, and uninspired sounding. Your ability to play faster and execute more intricate strumming patterns is severely weakened from bad tension. And furthermore, bad tension hurts. After all, playing ukulele should be fun and relaxing, not painful.

Because your brain is a powerful thing, it's important you think about being relaxed when you play ukulele and it's important you monitor your tension. However, you can't only tell yourself to relax. At least for me, whenever I try really hard to stay cool, loose, and limber, I can still end up just as tense. This is why it's important to take steps to condition your body towards a state of relaxation before you play. The warm up and relaxation exercises laid out in Chapter 1 are extremely beneficial in this way.

As you seek to become a better strummer (and a better ukulele player overall), pay attention to what your body is telling you. If it hurts, there is a better way. If you're not getting the speed and fluidity you want, don't be afraid to slow things down. Most of the time it's easier to play things slower without tension and gradually speed up than trying to come out of the gate at full speed. Additionally, keep your practice sessions at reasonable lengths and don't be discouraged if you need to take a break.

Rule #3: Strumming is intentional

Strumming is consistent, relaxed, and lastly, it's intentional. Whenever you play a song on the ukulele, a bunch of factors are at work that affect how the song is communicated. Some of the things that contribute to the overall sound, feel, and emotion of a song include:

- How you strum the ukulele (your strumming technique)
- Where you strum the ukulele (finding the sweet spot)
- What strumming pattern you use (rhythm)
- The speed of your playing (tempo)
- How loud or soft you are playing (dynamics)

A really cool way to think about these things is that they are ways to express yourself through the song with your ukulele. When you are intentional, you have an awareness of how you execute these things in your playing and you are seeking to improve each one through practice. This is because you realise these things affect how a song is communicated.

As with most things in life, the reality is that often you have to figure out what works best through trial and error. Before I can play how I mean to, I have to stumble around a little bit. When I want to learn a new song, I might have some initial gut reactions about what type of strumming works for that particular song, but a lot of times, I have to try new things and mess up. That one strumming pattern I learned for a previous song might not work for this new song I'm learning. In this way, as much as you could say strumming is intentional, it's also quite experimental.

One of the biggest mistakes you can make is being afraid of trying something new and failing. I've had students who are so afraid of making a mistake or developing bad habits that it sucks all of the joy and fun out of playing ukulele. I don't want this to happen to you. While you want to prevent bad habits, you're bound to develop some (I'm frequently fighting my own). It's not realistic to think you're going to do it all right from the start. Bad habits can always be fixed. Don't sweat it!

Finding the Right Strumming Pattern for Any Song

One of the best ways to put into practice the strumming techniques you are learning in this book is to learn a song that interests you. Find a chord chart of a song in a songbook or on the internet. Unfortunately, a standard chord chart doesn't usually give an indication of the strumming pattern or rhythm of a song. Normally, these charts just have the lyrics with chord symbols written over them. This means you have to use a little bit of ingenuity to find the right strumming pattern for the song.

Building a strumming repertoire

The first step in finding a strumming pattern that works for a song is to build a repertoire of strumming patterns. The exercises and patterns in this book are perfect for this because you can use them for a lot of different songs. As you work through these strumming patterns, you'll discover the best contexts in which to use them through your experimentation and practice of strumming actual songs in the pages ahead.

Many songs share the same strumming pattern, so don't be afraid to use a strumming pattern you've already mastered. It might not feel exciting to use that one strumming pattern you use all the time, but you can't be afraid to pull from what you know. Of course, you'll want to make sure whatever strumming pattern you use for a song works, but that leads us to the next point.

Listening to the song

Because a chord chart doesn't give you any indicator of what strumming pattern to use, you are going to have to rely on your ear. Even if you don't consider yourself to have the most musical ear, this is okay. A musical ear is something that can be developed with practice (that is, by listening).

With the internet, it's relatively easy to find a video performance of a song or to purchase a song from an online music store. Your goal is to listen to whatever song you want to learn over and over, and over again. When you're singing the song in your sleep, believe it or not, you're almost ready to play it!

Counting the song

In order to find the perfect strumming pattern for a song, you have to know how a song is counted. Of the songs we are interested in playing on the ukulele, 99.9 per cent of them have a specific count or *time signature*. Since rhythm is consistent, this count isn't going to change. It's going to repeat itself throughout an entire song almost all the time. If you know how a song is counted, you can easily create a strumming pattern on your own that fits within that count.

Most songs are counted in four beat measures or bars. This means throughout the entire song you can count 1, 2, 3, 4, and repeat. Some songs are also counted in three and six. These types of songs sound more like a waltz. As you listen to a song, clap your hands or tap your toes to find the beat. Count out loud to the song to try to find a count that fits. Remember, this count is a steady and consistent pulse that repeats.

You can figure out where to start your count by listening for the *downbeats* of a song. The downbeat is considered the first beat of a musical measure. So in a count of four, three, or six, beat one is the downbeat of the measure. It takes a little bit of practice to recognise downbeats by ear. Typically, chord changes happen on downbeats, and sections of a song, like a chorus or verse, begin on downbeats. Hearing the count of a song takes some practice, so don't be discouraged if you don't get it at first. Keep listening and tapping your foot. You'll also find that counting becomes easier as you work through the exercises and songs in this book.

Starting with down strums

Counting helps you understand and visualise the structure of a song. Ultimately, that allows you to create the perfect strumming pattern. Knowing how a song is counted is half the battle. Once you can count a song, you can pretty much play the song assuming you know the different chord positions indicated on the chord chart.

There is always one strumming pattern that works: down strums. Start with down strums as you're counting out loud. Even if you can't count and strum at the same time, it's better to get your feet wet and just start strumming. As you'll often find, sometimes what works might not actually be all that complicated. It's always best to start simple with a strumming pattern and add to it later to make it sound more interesting.

Knowing when to change chords

When you're looking at a song's chord chart, it can be challenging to know when to change chords. Most chord charts have the chords written above the lyrics in a way to indicate where the chords change as you're singing the song. However, this isn't always very accurate. In order to solve this, as you're listening and counting to the song, you need to listen for what beat the chords change in the song.

Most of the time chords change on the first beat of a measure – the downbeat. If they don't change on the first beat, then they probably will on the third beat. Don't be afraid to pick up your ukulele and experiment. Whenever you learn a new song, you have to rely on some trial and error.

Singing and Strumming at the Same Time

Singing and strumming at the same time can be difficult, because the rhythm of your strumming is often a little different from the rhythm of the vocal melody. This means you might strum on some beats that you don't sing, and vice versa. Getting the two to work together can take a little finesse. This can be a challenge for even seasoned ukulele players.

Playing the song through without singing

Before you can sing along with your strumming, you need to be comfortable with strumming a song and changing the chords without singing. This is very important. It's very hard to think about singing the right lyrics at the right pitch while you're thinking about the order of your strumming pattern. You want to work towards a place where you can strum without even thinking about it. This will free you up so you can focus on singing.

Humming first, singing later

You might find that humming a song under your breath while you strum is a good way to get a sense for how the melody of a song fits with the strumming. Humming is nice because you're not trying to remember the right lyrics or sound pretty. As you're humming and strumming, you might come across a chord change in the song that throws you off. When that happens, the best thing to do is to stop humming and play through the chord change until it feels more comfortable.

Simplifying isn't a bad thing

If you're finding that you still have trouble singing while you play the ukulele, it's always okay to simplify your strumming to just down strums and gradually build from there. Strumming is the foundation of a song, so it's always better to have a simple but strong strumming pattern versus one that is really complicated and all over the place. A solid, steady strumming pattern played with good timing will always work a hundred times better than a 'fancy' strumming pattern played out of time.

Chapter 4

Building a Repertoire of Strumming Patterns

In This Chapter

▶ Strumming more steadily, consistently and intentionally

▶ Unlocking thought processes to create captivating strumming patterns

▶ Learning how to apply strumming patterns to actual songs

To determine the right strumming pattern for a song you need to begin by building a repertoire of various strumming patterns that work in all sorts of different musical situations. As you do this, you gain the confidence to approach any song and figure out a strumming pattern that works. In this chapter, you learn a variety of highly practical strumming patterns that can be applied to literally thousands of different songs! Throughout the chapter, you use these patterns to learn just a few of these songs.

Even if you've been strumming for a while now, incorporate the exercises in this chapter into your practice routine to stretch, expand and refine your strumming even further. Through these exercises, you build your internal tempo clock to play a strumming pattern with confidence and consistency. Use the different ways of thinking about strumming in this chapter to unlock creative ways to approach a song's rhythm, so you can create your own strumming patterns beyond the pages of this book.

Believe it or not, eventually strumming becomes second nature as you learn to play ukulele. With time and repetition, your brain becomes used to different strumming movements – to the point where you don't have to actively think much about it. The less you have to think about your strumming the more mental energy you can devote towards other important aspects of playing your ukulele, like switching and playing chords or singing.

Discovering How to Use These Exercises to Become a Better Strummer

In your excitement, you might be tempted to blaze through all of the strumming pattern exercises and songs in this chapter in one sitting. To get the most out of these pattern exercises, it's best to go into this chapter with a little plan:

1. **From this chapter, just select a couple strumming pattern exercises to focus on per week. In your practice journal, write out which pattern exercises you are going to learn and write the date at the top of the page, so you can keep track of your progress.**

2. **Before playing a new pattern exercise, always spend time looking it over. Specifically, look at how the strums line up with the count.**

   Also, one of the biggest parts to these exercises is improving your ability to switch between chords, so be sure to look at any chords that are used in the exercise. If they are unfamiliar chords, practise the chord fingerings before trying to attempt the exercise.

3. **If available, listen to the audio associated with the pattern exercise. Hearing how a strumming pattern sounds is often easier than reading it off of a page.**

4. **Practise the pattern exercise at a slow tempo first and count out loud. If you have a metronome (I highly recommend it), for a slow tempo, set it anywhere from 60 to 84 BPM (beats per minute). Go slower if needed. Your goal is to play each exercise and switch between the chords without stopping.**

5. **When you can play the exercise at a slow tempo, speed up the tempo in small increments (5 to 10 BPM) to practise at faster speeds.**

If you have personal computer with a built-in microphone, or a smart phone that can record voice memos, try recording your strumming to hear how it sounds. Although this can be extremely humbling, it can help you identify weak areas of your strumming that you can improve.

You might find that as you go through these different strumming patterns you get some ideas for different ways of strumming that go beyond the pages of this book. If this happens, that's great; don't be afraid to experiment and try working out your own strumming patterns.

It might take a couple days, a week, or even longer to effortlessly perform each exercise. This is normal. It's important that you play it right at a slow speed. This allows you to easily fix any mistakes, so you're not repeating those when you speed things up. Be patient with yourself, because all of these exercises get easier with time, practice, and repetition!

To squeeze as many exercises as possible into these pages, most of the strumming pattern exercises are short and written in two-bar measures. To really strengthen your strumming, it's best to take the strumming pattern that is demonstrated and practise strumming it over the course of a minute or longer. In your practice journal, you might also write out different chord progressions to keep it fresh and to challenge your fingers.

Mastering the Universal Strumming Pattern

Before anything else, it's important you're comfortable counting out loud while you strum the ukulele. The count or *time signature* of a song is one of its most crucial aspects. All songs are structured around a consistent, steady, and repetitive count. If you know a song's count, you can easily build a strumming pattern around that count. In addition, counting out loud helps you build your internal timing clock, which makes your strumming less chaotic and more steady-sounding. These first couple of exercises get you comfortably counting and strumming at the same time.

Counting along with down strums

Different songs have different time signatures, but more often than not, songs are counted in measures or *bars* of four beats. This count of four is referred to as *common time* or 4/4 time signature.

The pattern exercise in the next figure is counted in four. Your goal is to make your strumming consistent in tempo and in tone. This means you want all of your strums to line up as closely as possible with your counting or metronome. Try your best to make all of the strums sound similar in volume and tone. Stay as loose and relaxed as possible, because any tension or strain works against you in the long run.

Track 11

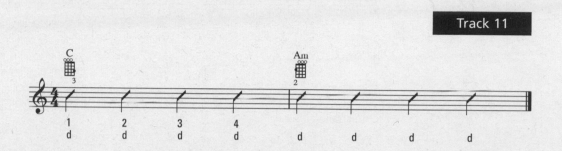

Strumming isn't about being fancy. You can perform the most complicated and fancy strumming pattern, but if it's not executed in consistent, steady timing, then you've completely defeated the purpose of strumming. Whenever you struggle with finding a strumming pattern that works for a song, start with down strums. A down strum pattern that's played with a good sense of timing is always better than a pattern that is more intricate but played out of time.

Keeping the beat with up strums

Just as you want your down strums to be consistent in timing and in tone, you also want this to be true of your up strums. As you practise the exercise in this figure, play it at a slow tempo, count out loud, and focus on lining up your up strums to the beat. Make your strums as consistent in volume and tone as possible.

Track 12

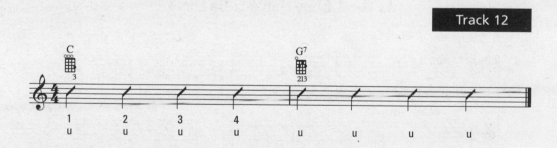

Combining down and up strums

The pattern exercise in the following figure uses both down and up strums to get you used to varying between different types of strums on different beats. Pay close attention to where the down and up strums fall on each beat, and again, intentionally think about making your strums consistent. Start slow at first, and then speed it up.

Track 13

Playing 'Mary Had a Little Lamb'

'Mary Had a Little Lamb' is a fantastic, simple song to get used to combining the count, strumming, and singing into playing an actual song. While you might not get nominated for a prestigious music award for your rendition of 'Mary Had a Little Lamb' (you never know, though), this song is a wonderful warm-up and exercise for the more challenging songs.

Take a look at the song's structure. Before trying to sing, strum through the song, while counting and focusing on keeping consistent timing. As you do this a few times, start to hum under your breath while you count to sense where the melody falls within the strumming. As you do that, you'll gain the confidence to sing out the song. Then, sing it loud and sing it strong!

Track 14

Mary Had a Little Lamb

Tackling Common Time Strumming Patterns

Since the vast majority of songs are counted in four, use the strumming pattern exercises in this section to equip yourself to play thousands of songs on the ukulele.

Developing eighth note strums

In the previous exercises, each strum received a quarter note in length – or, one beat. In the exercise in the following figure, each beat is divided into two eighth note strums containing a down strum and an up strum.

Track 15

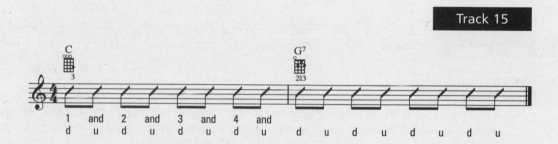

As you notice, down strums fall on the main beats of the measure – beats 1, 2, 3, and 4 – but in between each of these down strums, an up strum is added. Each quarter note beat is divided into two eighth notes. These up strums fall on what is sometimes referred to as the *offbeat*. Say the word 'and' to count the up strums between each of the down strums.

In the next two pieces, practise an all down-strum and all up-strum eighth note strumming pattern. For both exercises, count out loud and focus on making all of the strums sound consistent in tone, timing, and volume.

Track 16

Track 17

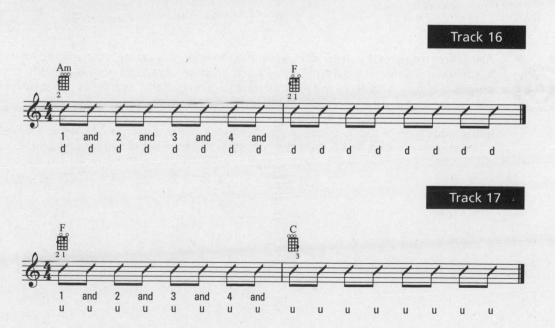

Building a multi-purpose strumming pattern

The following pattern exercises should be considered the most reliable and trusty strumming patterns in the book. They work in all different types of songs across various musical genres. Always have these in your back pocket!

In this exercise, combine quarter and eighth note strums to create a more interesting strumming pattern.

Track 18

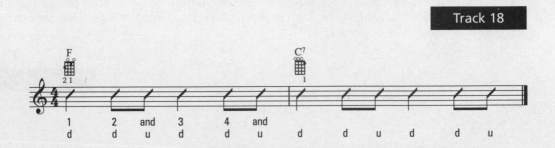

Create your own strumming pattern by changing around the order of down and up strums within the count. In the next figure, the quarter note strums now fall on the second and fourth beats with eighth note strums on the first and third beats.

Track 19

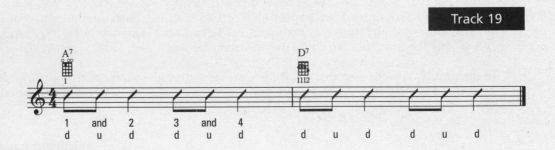

Just by rearranging the order of down and up strums, you create a strumming pattern that has its own unique feel and vibe. Using a combination of quarter note and eighth note strums is a great way to create your own strumming pattern. As long as you structure your pattern around a steady, consistent count, the sky is the limit!

In the same way, in the following piece, take the previous pattern exercises and shake 'em up a bit more to create a new strumming pattern over a four-bar chord progression.

Track 20

Practising chord changes on different beats

In the exercises so far, chord changes have happened on the first beat of the measure – also known as the *downbeat*. In a song, it's extremely common for chord changes to happen on the downbeat, however, to be prepared for any situation, it's very important to practise changing chords on other beats too.

The second most common place for chords to change in a song is on the third beat of a measure. In 4/4 time signature, the third beat is the second strongest beat after the downbeat. Practise the next exercise to strengthen your ability to change chords in the middle of a measure.

Track 21

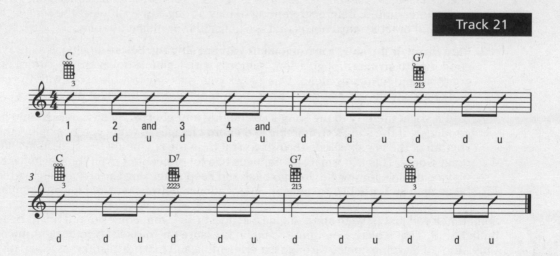

Sometimes chords consecutively change on multiple beats in a measure to create a musical walk up or walk down. Try your hand at playing the following piece to hear how this sounds.

Track 22

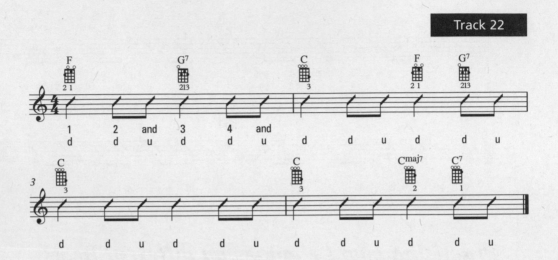

Playing 'Jingle Bells'

By now, you have quite a few strumming patterns under your belt. Practising these strumming patterns is one thing but getting them to work within the context of a song that isn't 'Mary Had a Little Lamb' can sometimes be the hardest part.

Whenever I approach learning a new song, I like to always follow these three steps:

1. **Familiarise your fingers with the chords used in the song.** Your ability to anticipate chords changes in a song is essential to keeping your strumming consistent, steady and uninterrupted. Before attempting to play a song, always look at the song's chord chart and practise any chords that are unfamiliar or difficult to play.

2. **Play through the song's arrangement without singing.** Before singing, it's always a good idea to strum through a song's chords with a simple down strum pattern, while counting and humming along. This allows you to fix any trouble spots with the count and chords without having to worry about remembering the right lyrics.

3. **Add a vocal melody to the song's strumming and chords.** By now, you should have a good idea of the song's strumming and chord changes. If while you're singing, the rhythm of the vocal melody throws you off from the rhythm of the strumming pattern, don't worry: This is normal and happens to a lot of people – even those who've been playing ukulele for awhile. Just go back and keep practising the strumming pattern. It takes time and practice to develop independence between strumming and singing.

Sometimes you just have to start singing a song and see what comes out. It might be pretty – it might not. That's okay. Don't put too much pressure on yourself to get it right the first time. A lot of learning comes through experimenting and making mistakes, so be patient with yourself.

To play the famous Christmas song 'Jingle Bells,' use any of the strumming patterns you've learned so far or have created on your own that are structured around a count of four. For this song, I like to use a strumming pattern from earlier in the chapter, but if that's too difficult, simplify the strumming pattern with all down strums and build from there.

Jingle Bells

Track 23

Making Common Time Strumming Patterns More Interesting

With just the strumming patterns you've practised so far, you already know some really strong patterns that can be used to play a wide variety of songs. Still though, there are even more ways you can spice up your strumming.

Accenting the beat

An *accented* beat is one that is emphasised or played slightly louder than others. Accents are a tool you can use to change the entire feel of a strumming pattern and add more character and life to your rhythms.

Here, practise accenting the first and third beats of the measure. Accented beats are represented by a '>' mark above the beat.

Track 24

 Avoid tensing up or clenching your strumming hand as you practice accenting strums. To accent a beat, it just takes a slight bit more of contact from your strumming hand's fingers to the ukulele's strings. If you struggle with tension, take time to relax, slow down the tempo, and come back to it.

 To make accents more noticeable, strum the unaccented, normal beats a little more softly. If you tend to have a heavy hand and strum really loudly, relax a little bit to allow room for the accented beats to stand out.

After you get the feel for that, try adding in some up-strums to the pattern and accent the first and third beats of the measure.

Track 25

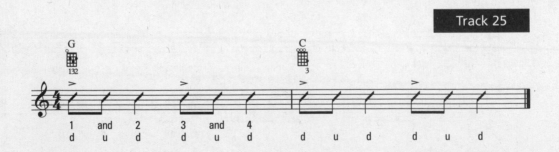

Now, change around which beats are accented. You can change the entire feel of a strumming pattern by changing which strums are accented. In the next exercise, practise accenting the second and fourth beats of the measure.

Track 26

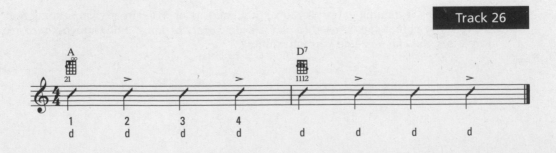

In the next exercise, take a normal strumming pattern and accent the down strums that fall right on the second and fourth beats. In 4/4 time signature, these beats are known as the *backbeats*.

Track 27

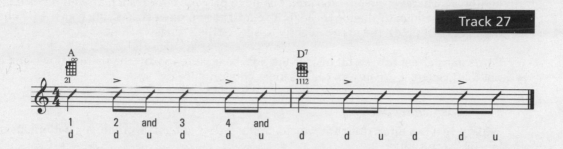

Entire genres of music have been created by the way beats are accented. For example, in country, Hawaiian, pop, and rock music, the backbeat is almost always accented. As you play different strumming patterns, you can't go wrong with accenting the backbeat.

Using syncopation in three different ways

Syncopation is a word used to describe accents on beats that aren't normally stressed in a rhythm. Syncopated rhythms find themselves in all sorts of music but tend to be most noticeable in jazz, funk, reggae, Hawaiian, blues and pop music.

Believe it or not, in the previous section you played some syncopated rhythms by accenting the backbeats. In 4/4 time signature, beats 1 and 3 are the strongest. So by accenting beats 2 and 4, you created syncopation.

To make things more complex, and therefore, more interesting to listen to, go even farther and emphasise beats that don't fall on beat 1, 2, 3, or 4. I show you how to do this in the following exercises, so you can really start to tap into the power of syncopation!

Missed beat syncopation

What you don't play on the ukulele is often just as important as what you do play. By choosing not to strum certain beats, you add tension to a strumming pattern and draw your listener in. To put this into action, add a *rest* to make a dramatic statement in your strumming.

Track 28

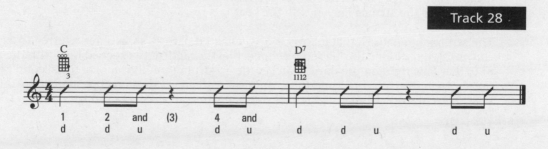

In this piece, silence or mute the strings to perform a musical *rest* on the third beat. The little squiggly-looking note representing the third beat is known as a quarter rest. Because the third beat in 4/4 time signature is a strong beat, the absence of this beat creates syncopation.

To silence the strings for a rest, you have two options. The first way is to use your strumming hand to lightly lay your palm across the strings. The second way is to use your fretting hand. How you silence the strings with your fretting hand depends on what chord you're playing. If there are a lot of open strings in the chord, such as the C chord in this exercise, lightly lay whatever fingers you aren't using to play the chord, such as your index finger, across the strings to silence them. If the chord has no open strings, such as the D7 chord in the figure, lift up off the chord slightly to silence the strings.

Performing a rest takes a bit of coordination, so be sure to slow the pattern down and count out loud. Speed it up only as you get more comfortable.

Suspended syncopation

While a rest is a more dramatic way to create syncopation in a strumming pattern, using a *tie* is a bit more subtle.

Track 29

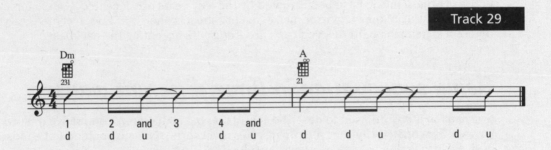

In this exercise, the curved line that connects the eighth note on the 'and' of two and the quarter note of beat three is known as a *tie*. In the context of strumming, whenever you see a tie, hold the strum for the duration of the tied notes.

As you can see, the tied notes are an eighth note and a quarter note, which equals one and a half beats in duration. This means you let the up strum on the 'and' of the second beat ring out all the way through the third beat. Even though you're not strumming the third beat, it's still a good idea to count it, so you don't get off time.

Offbeat syncopation

Eliminating down strums from beats 1, 2, 3, or 4 and emphasising the up strums on the 'and' of these beats, or the offbeat, is a great way to create different syncopated feels. Because down strums are removed from the following patterns, these patterns begin to get more challenging than the previous. Be sure to count these out and play them at a slow speed first to sense where the strums line up with the beat.

The strumming pattern that follows is a syncopated pattern sometimes referred to as the *calypso* strum. Notice the curved tie connecting the 'and' of the second beat with the eighth note that falls right on the third beat. Let the up strum from the 'and' of the second beat ring out through the third beat, and then, continue with an up strum on the 'and' of the third beat. The calypso strum is highly versatile and works in all sorts of songs.

Track 30

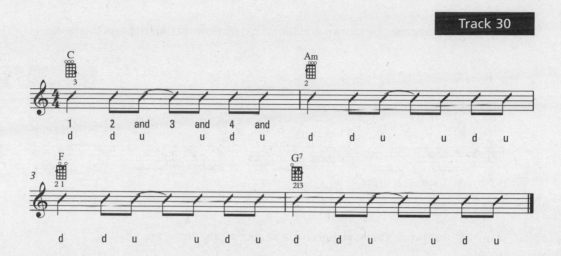

Rearranging up strums to create different feels

When you emphasise the offbeat in your strumming, you're able to create some really interesting rhythms, but this also presents a challenge because it tends to be easier to recognise the main beats. The following pattern exercises challenge your internal timing clock and get you used to feeling the offbeat.

In the next exercise, there is no down strum on the second beat of the measure, just an up strum on the 'and' of the second beat of the measure.

Track 31

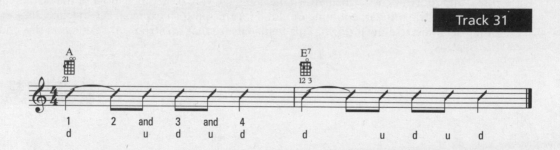

The next piece switches things around a little bit by removing a down strum from the fourth beat and keeping an up strum on the 'and' of the fourth beat.

Track 32

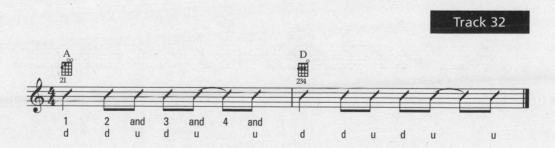

In the next exercise, beats two and four have no down strum right on the beat.

Track 33

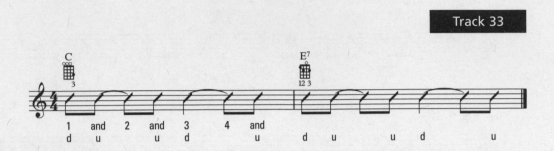

For the next piece, down strums from beats two and three are missing.

Track 34

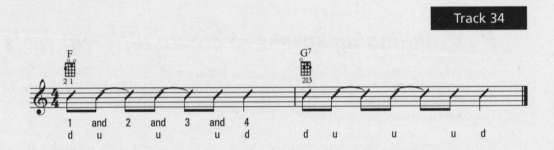

The pattern exercise in the next figure doesn't include any down strums on the second, third, and fourth beats. This pattern has a reggae vibe to it. Since most of the strumming happens on the offbeat, counting out loud for this pattern exercise is especially important. Don't be afraid to slow it down. This helps ensure that up strums are falling on the 'and' of the beat.

Track 35

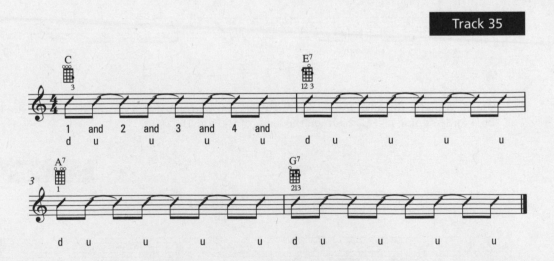

Playing 'I've Been Working On the Railroad'

The song 'I've Been Working On the Railroad' is counted in four. This means you can use any of the strumming patterns you've practised so far to play this song. I like to use the calypso strumming pattern from earlier in the chapter.

Take note that in the second to last measure there is a chord change on the third beat. Since there is no down strum on the third beat of the calypso strum, accommodate this chord change by breaking the calypso strumming pattern and strumming down through the third beat.

Track 36

I've Been Working On the Railroad

Waltzing Along with 3/4 Time Signature Strumming Patterns

To play a waltz strumming pattern on the ukulele, you're required to structure your strumming around a completely different time signature or way of counting. Practicing strumming patterns in different time signatures is important because it allows you to find the right strumming pattern for all sorts of songs.

A waltz is played in 3/4 time signature, where there are three counted beats per measure. While the waltz is commonly used to learn 3/4 time signatures, this time signature also finds itself in other musical styles like marches, hymns, country ballads, and Hawaiian music.

For these pattern exercises, count out loud: 1, 2, 3. Focus on making your strumming as consistent and as steady with this count as possible.

Practising versatile 3/4 strumming patterns

Check out the exercise that follows. This is a simple quarter note down strum pattern played to a count of three. To give it that waltz feel, accent the first beat by strumming it louder than the other beats. More often than not, this basic strumming pattern gets the job done for most waltzes.

Track 37

In the next piece, take the previous pattern exercise and make it a bit more interesting by adding some up strums in between the down strums.

Track 38

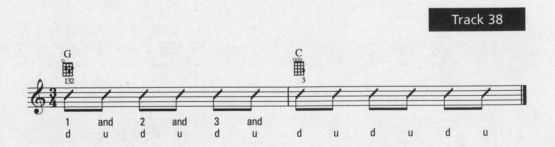

In this exercise, use all down strums to give the pattern a driving feel, while turning the strumming pattern back around by inserting a nice up strum on the 'and' of the third beat.

Track 39

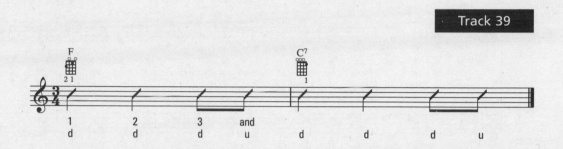

Strumming patterns in 3/4 time signature can also be syncopated. In this piece, the down strum on the second beat is left out; so there is only an up strum on the 'and' of the second beat.

Track 40

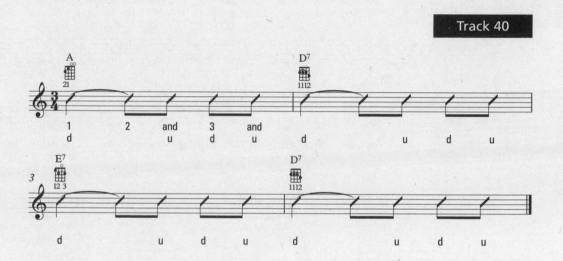

Playing 'Oh My Darling, Clementine'

'Oh My Darling, Clementine' is a well-loved, must-know ukulele classic written in 3/4 time signature. The 'waltzy' feel of this song gives it a very entertaining and happy sound despite its morbid lyrics. For this song, I like to use the driving strumming pattern from the previous section, however, have fun trying any of the other strumming patterns you've learned or created in 3/4 time signature.

Track 41

Oh My Darling, Clementine

Getting More Advanced with 6/8 Time Signature Strumming Patterns

There's still another way some songs are counted. In 6/8 time signature, there are six counted beats per measure, where each beat is represented by an eighth note. This is different from 4/4 and 3/4 time signature where each beat is represented by a quarter note. The primary accent in 6/8 time signature happens on the first beat, with a secondary accent on the fourth beat. These beats are accented to create a rhythmic pulse.

Don't worry if the technicalities that separate these different time signatures don't make much sense at first. At the end of the day, what matters most to you should be how these rhythms sound in actual songs. All this underlying theory is quite beneficial to know and gives us a way to talk about music with each other, but it's often very nuanced, almost to the point where it can become annoying and even discouraging if it doesn't 'click' right away.

In my experience, I've found that all the music theory stuff tends to be fleshed out as you spend more and more time actually playing the ukulele in different ways. Don't let the mumbo-jumbo of music theory ever discourage from making some beautiful. Some of the greatest musicians dead and alive hardly knew a lick of music theory!

Developing delightful 6/8 strumming patterns

To start off, practise this all eighth note down strum pattern exercise. Be sure to count out loud: 1, 2, 3, 4, 5, 6. Practice making your down strums line up with each count. To create a pulse to the strumming pattern, accent beats 1 and 4 by strumming them a little bit harder than the other strums.

Track 42

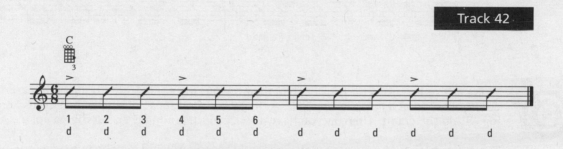

After getting used to just down strums, add up strums in between your down strums, as shown in the figure which follows. You'll notice the rhythm notation for this exercise looks a little different. Because each counted beat receives an eighth note in 6/8 time signature, when you split these beats into a down strum and a up strum, you end up with a sixteenth note down strum and a sixteenth note up strum. Be sure to go slow at first to sense how this is counted.

Track 43

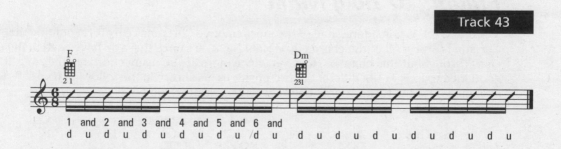

If you want to add even more variety to a 6/8 strumming pattern, be more selective with where you place up strums. For the pattern exercise in the next figure, add up strums in between the down strums for the first three counts, but then, for the last three counts, play just down strums.

Track 44

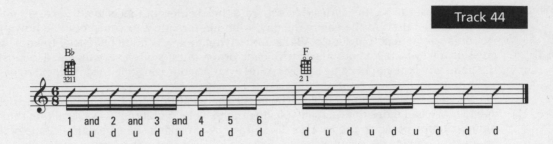

To take things even further, in the following piece, notice how there is no down strum played on the fifth count but there is an up strum that is played on the 'and' of the fifth count.

Track 45

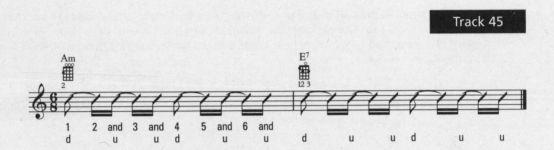

This pattern is quite a bit trickier than the previous ones. To get the hang of this exercise, count out loud at a *very* slow speed first to get a strong sense of where the strums are falling within the count. Then, as you have a sense for it, gradually speed things up.

The other trick to this pattern is to constantly keep your hand moving in a down and up motion, as you practised a couple of pieces back. While maintaining this motion throughout the strum, raise your strumming hand slightly as to not hit the strings for the down strums on the second, third, fifth, and sixth beats. This idea is more felt than followed exactly, so as you practise, experiment, and spend time with 6/8 time signatures, work towards getting the feel of constantly keeping a loose and steady motion as you strum.

Playing 'O Holy Night'

'O Holy Night' is considered one of the most emotive Christmas carols recounting the Christmas story. All of the chords in 'O Holy Night' are ones that you have used in the exercises throughout this chapter. However, since there are so many chords in the song, it's a good idea to look at the different chord positions, as shown in the following figure. Practise changing between these chords before trying to play the song.

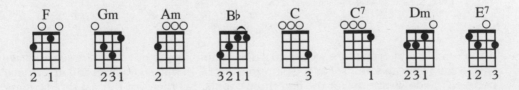

Use any of the 6/8 strumming patterns you learned to play 'O Holy Night.' I like to use a simple down strum pattern. I find that if I use a more complicated pattern, it sounds too busy and takes away from the words. To really capture the intensity of the chorus, you might strum louder than in the verses.

Track 46

O Holy Night

Chapter 5

Taking Strumming Patterns to a Higher Level

....

In This Chapter

▶ Creating a strumming pattern that 'feels' good

▶ Practising faster, more complex strumming patterns

▶ Using dynamics to create a moving performance

▶ Improving chord changes

....

Chapter 4 shows you how to build a solid repertoire of strumming patterns that can be used in all different types of songs. You create different strumming patterns around a specific, steady count, and build your internal tempo clock by counting out loud and even practising with a metronome. Strumming the ukulele with consistent timing is crucial, but there are other important aspects that help make your strumming even stronger and more interesting for your listener.

In this chapter, you take your strumming even further by swinging the rhythm, strum faster, more complex patterns, use the power of dynamics in your playing, and improve chord changes. By honing in on these nuances, you're able to create a compelling performance for your listener.

Getting Groovy with Shuffle Rhythms

The shuffle rhythm is all about getting the music to feel good. This musical feel is better known as the *groove*. Musical styles like the blues, jazz, funk, Hawaiian, gospel, reggae, and hip hop are all about the groove that comes from a shuffle rhythm.

For example, take the basic eighth note down and up strumming pattern in this exercise:

Track 47

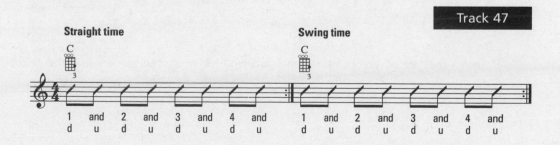

In normal, 'Straight time', the down strum is equal in length to the up strum. However, in a shuffle rhythm or 'Swing time', the down strum is held twice as long in duration as the up strum. This unequal duration between down and up strums is referred to as *swing*. Depending on how hard you're 'swinging' the beat, this duration varies.

To keep things simple, in this book, shuffle rhythms are written the same way as a normal, straight rhythm, with the exception of the words 'Swing time' written at the top of the music. A shuffle rhythm should have a pulse that makes you want to tap your foot or bob your head to the beat. You still count a swung strumming pattern in 4/4 time signature the same way – *1 and, 2 and, 3 and, 4 and* – but out loud, you sound out the number counts longer than you say the 'and' counts.

To practise a shuffle rhythm, at a slow tempo, use the strumming pattern in the first exercise to alternate between a straight rhythm and a shuffle rhythm. Listen to the audio track to hear the differences between each one. Notice how I'm still playing in time, but I'm making the pattern sound less rigid and more loose when I start playing in swing time.

Listening to music is one of the best practice exercises. If you struggle with the shuffle rhythm, take a couple of days to listen to that old blues and jazz music that's been collecting dust on your shelf. This always helps me get in the right mindset to feel the groove.

Finding the pocket with shuffle rhythm exercises

When you're playing with a consistent, steady groove, you're playing 'in the pocket.' To develop this groove, in the following exercises take the strumming patterns in Chapter 4 and apply a shuffle rhythm.

For these strumming exercises, practise switching between straight and swing time at a slow to medium tempo (78–94 BPM, if you have a metronome). Be sure to listen to the audio track with each exercise to hear the differences between the two.

There doesn't have to be constant down and up strums to play a shuffle rhythm feel. For the next exercise, take a regular strumming pattern and swing the beat.

Track 48

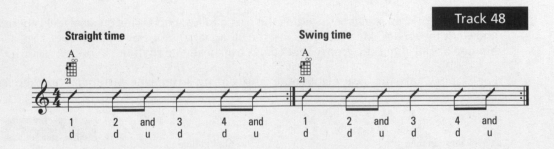

Patterns that are played in swing time can also be syncopated, as shown in the next figure.

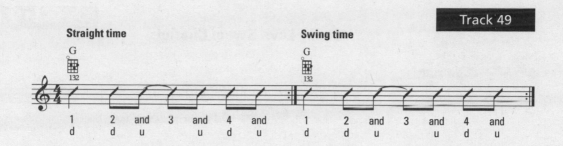

Track 49

In the next exercise, there is no down strum on beat two. Notice how the quarter note down strum on beat one combined with the syncopation and swung time creates a little bit of tension in the pattern.

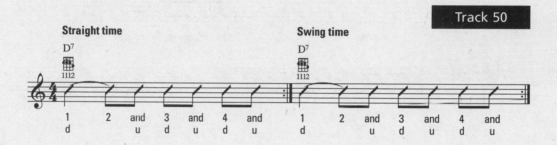

Track 50

Playing shuffle rhythms isn't limited to the patterns above. Take any of the strumming patterns you've learned in this book or have created on your own and practise applying a 'swing time' feel.

Playing 'Swing Low, Sweet Chariot'

To play 'Swing Low, Sweet Chariot', use any of the swung strumming patterns in this chapter or ones you've created to play this song.

Track 51

Strumming Faster without Getting Sloppier

The energy of a song is largely tied to the tempo of the song. More lively toe-tapping tunes require a quicker strumming pattern. In this section, improve your strumming speed, while still sounding smooth and steady.

Working on relaxing strumming movements

The biggest inhibitor to strumming fast is tension. At first, the idea of playing fast can be a little overwhelming and seem impossible, so the temptation is to overcompensate the effort by trying *really hard* to strum fast. Unfortunately, putting this pressure on yourself is counterproductive because it usually results in unwanted tension that slows you down.

Playing fast is as much as a feeling as it is a skill. To develop the feeling of strumming fast, use the following exercise:

1. **Start by strumming down and up across the strings at a slow, relaxed speed.**

2. **In a 'burst' no longer than a couple seconds, strum as fast as you can.**

3. **Bring your speed back down and repeat the exercise.**

The goal in this exercise is to stay as relaxed and 'sloppy' in your strumming as possible through the entire exercise, even during the bursts of speed. There isn't a magical speed to achieve with this exercise. This exercise is beneficial because it gets you used to the feeling of playing fast without worrying about your timing or sounding pretty.

 Strumming fast tends to work best when you're trying the least. Ensuring that your strumming hand is relaxed and free from tension is essential to being able to play faster and more complicated strumming rhythms. If you struggle with getting your strumming hand and fingers to relax, don't hesitate to return to Chapter 1 to work through some of the stretches and warm up exercises.

Minimizing wasted strumming motion

If strumming fast is about trying to exert the least amount of effort as possible, one of the best ways to waste energy on strumming is to over exaggerate the strumming motion.

 On down strums, avoid strumming way past the bottom string, and on up strums, avoid strumming way past the top string. Think about strumming in a smaller space. Reducing the space, movement, and time between down strums and up strums reduces the effort required to move your strumming hand across the strings. This translates into added speed.

Drawing up a plan to improve strumming speed

One of the most important things to keep in mind about strumming fast is that it's never random – it always fit within the context of good timing (a song's count or time signature). Strumming fast, like strumming slow, sounds best when it's intentional and controlled.

To get to that point, follow these three steps to start increasing your strumming speed:

1. **Before picking up the ukulele, always stretch, relax, and work towards ridding yourself of any tension in your strumming hand.**

2. **Select a basic strumming pattern you're familiar with and practise it at a slow to medium tempo (78–108 BPM, if you have a metronome).**

3. **In small increments (5–10 BPM), gradually increase the tempo to play the strumming pattern faster.**

 Never sacrifice consistency in a strumming pattern for speed. If a faster tempo is too hard to practise, don't be discouraged. Slow it down and practise at a slower tempo. As that slower tempo becomes easier and more relaxed, it'll make the faster tempo easier in the future.

Here are a couple strumming patterns you can apply the above plan to. Listen to the audio with each exercise to hear it played at a fast tempo. If you have a metronome, make it your goal to play the following patterns at 168 BPM in a steady, consistent rhythm.

To start out, work on increasing your strumming speed for a basic down and up strumming pattern, as shown in below. You might try accenting beats two and four and swinging the beat to create a nice, toe-tappin' pulse. Keep your hand and fingers as loose as possible.

Track 52

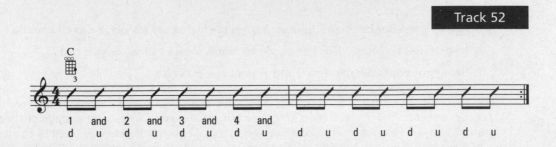

In the next exercise, take a common syncopated strumming pattern and speed it up.

Track 53

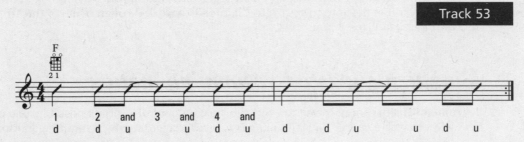

 Go back to Chapter 4 and use the above plan for strumming fast to develop your speed for other strumming patterns.

Playing 'Hello! Ma Baby'

'Hello! Ma Baby' is a fun, upbeat song that requires a faster, toe-tappin' strumming pattern. Before playing the song, take a look at the chords used in this song in the following figure. There is a new chord used in this song: F°7. The letter 'F' with the superscript circle and the '7' is called an *F diminished seventh chord*.

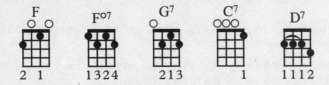

 For this song, I use a basic strumming pattern, but I swing the rhythm and accent beats two and four to really give it that toe-tapping pulse. It's okay if you need to slow down the tempo as you're first learning the song. As you get more comfortable with the chord changes, speed it up.

Hello! Ma Baby

Showing Off Subdivided Strumming Patterns

Some songs are just fast in tempo, so they require a strumming pattern that's played fast (see 'Hello! Ma Baby'). Makes sense. However, some songs are played at a slow to medium tempo, but there are quick, fast strums added to make what otherwise would be a simple strumming pattern sound really interesting. Here's a couple of ways to do this.

Souping up your strumming with sixteenth notes

Some songs are slow to mid-tempo, but the strumming pattern is modified to insert quick, fast strums that add interest to the strumming pattern. When a beat in a strumming pattern is modified like this to add fast strums, it is *subdivided*.

A subdivided beat is one that is divided up into multiple shorter note lengths that sound faster when played. For example, if you take one quarter note strum and divide it, you get two eighth note strums. Furthermore, if you take one eighth note strum and divide it, you get two sixteenth note strums.

This sounds more complicated than it really is. The pattern in the next exercise takes a down and up strumming pattern and subdivides the second and fourth beats into four sixteenth notes each played with alternating down and up strums. This exercise is repeated once, as indicated by the repeat sign at the end of the exercise.

Track 55

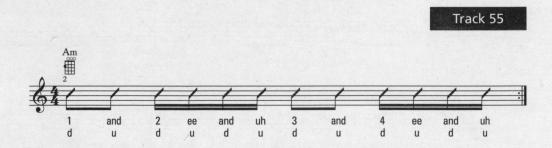

Start to practise this pattern at a slow tempo (60 BPM) and gradually speed it up. While this is a pretty slow tempo, as you can see, when you play this pattern, the sixteenth notes go by quickly. By adding in sixteenth notes to a normal strumming pattern, you can make part of the strumming pattern sound fast, even though you aren't speeding anything up in terms of the actual overall tempo.

Sometimes though, a song is played fast and there are added sixteenth notes to make it sound even faster. For example, listen to the next track. The core strumming pattern is a basic pattern, but the fourth beat is subdivided into sixteenth notes. If you play this at a moderate speed (100-120 BPM), these sixteenth note strums happen pretty quickly, which creates quite a bit of flavor to the pattern.

Track 56

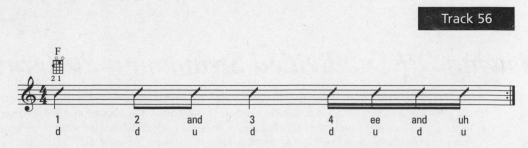

Don't forget to breathe, relax, and stay loose. Again, as you practise these exercises, start slow at first and only work up to a faster tempo in small increments.

Trying out triplet strums

Subdividing a rhythm into triplets is an excellent way to break up the monotony of a basic strumming pattern. Triplets find themselves in Hawaiian strumming as well as many other musical genres.

As the name implies, triplets are formed when you take a quarter note strum and subdivide it into a group of three strums called a *triplet*. In a 4/4 time signature, count a triplet by saying: *one - trip - let, two - trip - let, three - trip - let, four - trip - let*.

To strum a triplet, first, strum *down* across the strings with your index finger. Think about flicking your index finger across the string, while keeping a loose hand and wrist, because on the 'trip' of the beat, your thumb needs to be immediately ready to strum *down* across the strings again. On the 'let' of the beat, strum *up* with your index finger. For these movements, you might find it more natural to substitute the index finger with your middle finger.

In the next exercise, practise counting and strumming triplets to a count of four. Count out loud at a slow speed first to sense how the triplets fit within the beat. To perfect your triplet technique and get faster, increase the speed of this exercise a little bit at a time.

Track 57

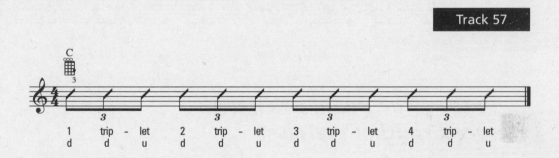

In the next exercise, incorporate a triplet into a basic down and up strumming pattern. The fourth beat of the strumming pattern is a triplet strum.

Track 58

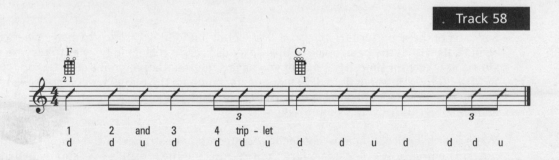

Try moving the triplet around to the first beat as shown in the next figure.

Track 59

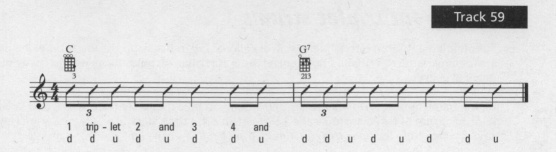

In a song, you might decide to add triplet strums to multiple beats. In this exercise, add triplets to the first and third beats.

Track 60

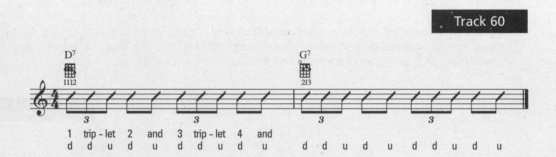

Putting the pedal down with speed rhythm exercises

The following speed rhythm exercises stretch your ability to incorporate fast sixteenth note and triplet strums into your playing. While these exercises are not intended to be used as a core strumming pattern for a song, these exercises do challenge your sense of timing and make you a better, more controlled and intentional strummer. In the audio tracks, each of these exercises is repeated once. Repeat the patterns in these exercises multiple times as you practise.

For each of these pattern exercises, at first, count out loud *very slowly* to sense where each strum falls within the beat. Some of these exercises are a real mind-boggler to play, so go slow and take your time. After that, if you have a metronome, set it at a slow tempo (40–70 BPM), and then, in small 5–10 BPM increments, bump up the tempo to increase speed. If at any point you notice tension in your strumming hand, stop, take a break, and come back to it another time, starting at a slower tempo.

In the next exercise, there are consecutive sixteenth note strums for the second and third beats. The first beat receives a quarter note strum and the fourth beat is subdivided into eighth note strums.

Track 61

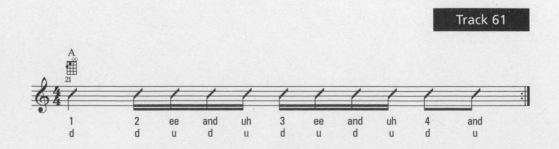

To spice things up, the pattern exercise in the next exercise creates a little bit of syncopation along with some sixteenth note strums.

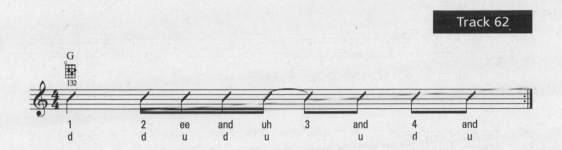

This exercise gets creative with sixteenth notes by removing the sixteenth note up strum on the 'ee' of the fourth beat. This is a really cool rhythm to add to any strumming pattern, but this can be challenging movement to coordinate, so count out loud *very* slowly at first to sense where the strums fall within the beat.

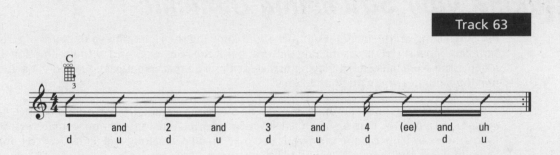

For the next exercise, take a regular syncopated strumming pattern and add a triplet strum on the second beat.

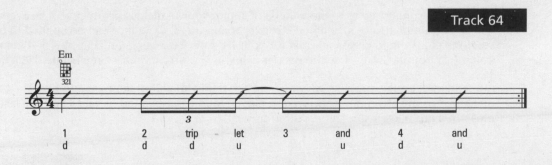

Just when you think it couldn't get any crazier, the next pattern exercise combines sixteenth notes with triplets. This is a hard exercise to get down, so again, start slow and break the pattern into small pieces.

Track 65

F

| | | | | | | | | |
1   2   ee   and uh   3   and   4   trip - let
d   d   u   d   u   u   d   d   u

 Sixteenth note and triplet strums add a nice rhythmic touch to any strumming pattern. This creates interest and sounds impressive to your listener. Being able to play fast in good timing takes a lot of practice and coordination, so if you're not getting the speed you want, be patient with yourself and continue to incorporate these exercises into your practice routine. With time and dedication, you will see improvement.

Making Your Strumming Dynamic

Playing a song on the ukulele isn't just about knowing the right pattern or order of strums. You can know the right strumming pattern, but if the song is played without emotion and feeling, the song falls short. Playing ukulele isn't just a mathematical equation – it's about making a connection with your listener!

A powerful way to inject emotion and feeling into your strumming is through the use of *dynamics*. Dynamics help a song tell a story by creating tension and musical interest. Use the following exercises to hone in on your use of dynamics in a song and learn how to implement them in a way that allows the song to tell a story.

Playing loudly and softly

The term *dynamics* refers to the volume of sound your ukulele is producing. Like accents, where certain beats are strummed stronger than others, dynamics can be applied to entire sections of a song to create interest for your listener. You can hear examples of dynamics of volume in popular songs like the Beatles' 'Hey Jude' and Nirvana's 'Smells Like Teen Spirit'.

In the next exercise, practise varying between loud and soft in your strumming. The first two measures of the strumming pattern are played loud (represented by an *f*), and the last two measures are played soft (represented by a *p*).

Track 66

C

f   *p*
d   d u d d u

 To strum louder, think about 'digging' into the strings harder with your strumming fingers. Imagine strumming down into the ukulele to get the strings to really snap. To strum softer, strum so your fingers barely graze the top of the strings.

Don't be tricked: Strumming louder does not equal strumming faster, and strumming softer does not equal strumming slower. If you have a metronome, use it to ensure you're still keeping a steady tempo.

Your use of dynamics doesn't need to be as dramatic as in the last exercise to be effective. For some parts of a song, you can gradually get louder and softer. In the next exercise, for the first two measures, gradually increase the volume of your strumming, and for the last two measures, gradually decrease the volume.

Track 67

d   d u d   d u

Use dynamics to give a song a sense of journey. For example, in songs that have a verse and chorus, you might make the verse quieter than the chorus to give the chorus more impact and energy.

Dynamics are relative. In order for dynamics to be effective, there needs to be variation in volume between certain parts of a song. If you're always playing loud, it doesn't necessarily mean that you're adding energy to the song. It could just mean that it sounds loud and it hurts your listener's ears. To make dynamics effective, be more intentional about holding back in certain parts of a song to draw your listener in. This way, when you get to parts that require more emphasis, you have the ability to get louder.

Varying rhythmic complexity

The volume of your playing isn't the only way to insert emotion into your playing. A great way to give a song a sense of movement is by varying your strumming for certain sections or parts of a song.

For example, in a verse, try simplifying your strumming pattern. To do that, you might take out certain up strums and make it more sparse and less busy. Then, in a chorus, make your strumming pattern busier and more complicated by adding in more up strums, creating syncopation, or throwing in some fast sixteenth note or triplet strums. This sort of contrast in rhythm allows a song to move and progress in a way that tells a story. The best way to demonstrate this is to play a song.

'Oh! Susanna'

For 'Oh! Susanna,' simplify the verse to just down strums. In addition, hold back a little bit, so the volume of the verse is quieter than the chorus. Then, when the chorus kicks in, strum a little louder, and strum a more complex strumming pattern to really lift the energy off the ground.

By adding in dynamics to the song, you really have the ability to draw your listener into the story of the song. It takes this song from being a standard ole folk song to being a really fun and engaging performance.

Oh! Susanna

Track 68

Recognising Offbeat Chord Changes

So far, most of the chord changes for the songs in this book have happened on the first or the third beats of the measure. However, in some songs, chord changes happen on the 'and' of a beat. Chords that change on the 'and' of a beat can feel rushed or hurried to the ear, although they are still done in good timing.

Switching to chords on offbeats

The following four bar chord progressions help you get used to feeling offbeat chord changes in different scenarios. As you practise these, you'll be able to more easily recognize these when listening to a song.

First, practise changing chords on the 'and' of the second beat, as shown in the next figure.

Track 69

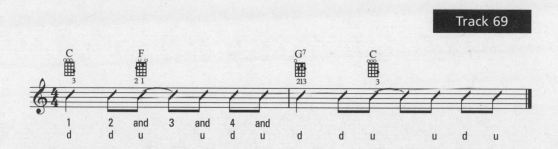

In this exercise, practise changing chords on the 'and' of the fourth beat. Typically, it's expected that a chord changes on the first beat of the measure, so when the chord changes on the 'and' of the fourth beat, it can sound rushed to the ear, even though it's still played in good timing.

Track 70

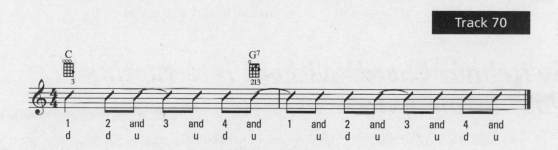

Variation on the 12-bar blues

The 12-bar blues is a great, practical example of chords that change on the 'and' of the beats. For this variation of the 12-bar blues (for more variations on the 12-bar blues, check out *Ukulele For Dummies, 1st Edition*), use the following chords, as shown in the next figure:

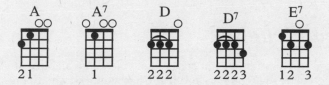

To make the change between D and D7 easier, for the D chord, barre the top three strings on the 2nd fret with your middle finger. Bend your finger back to avoid muting the bottom string. Then, to play the D7 chord, maintain the same position for the D chord but place your ring or little finger on the 3rd fret of the bottom string.

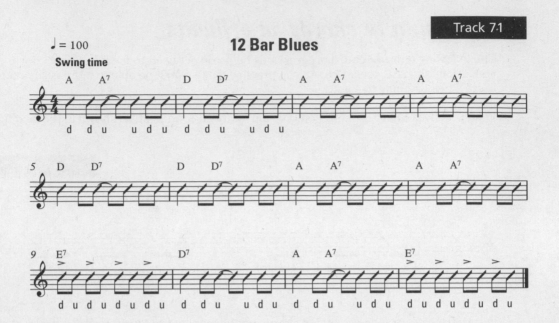

Track 7·1

When you're playing a song or a chord progression like the 12-bar blues, don't forget to use dynamics and think about telling a story. For example, in measure 9 and 12 of the previous exercise, I accent the main beats for the E7 chord as if I wanted to make a statement. While it's not a big change in the strumming pattern, that little bit of variety really gives the song character than if I were to just strum through those parts like normal.

Switching Chords without Interrupting Your Strumming

Improving your ability to change chords is an essential part towards becoming a better strummer. Yet, there are just some chords that are a real doozy to play. A chord that buzzes or doesn't ring out has the ability to throw your strumming completely off.

In Chapter 4, I talked about how it's important to practise chord changes separate from strumming. Whenever you learn a new chord, your fingers need time and practise to put the chord into muscle memory. Beyond that though, even when you know how to play a chord, there are some tricks that allow you to switch chords with greater ease to keep your strumming consistent and steady.

Setting up a chord change

Always set up a chord change when switching chords. When you set up a chord change, you're considering the chord you're switching to and from, and you're trying to find a way to play both chords so you barely have to move your fingers between each chord.

For example, in the next exercise the pattern changes between an Em and a G chord.

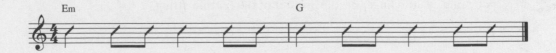

Typically, the Em and G chords' finger positions are notated as in the next figure.

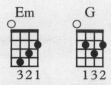

This is a standard position for these chords. Yet, in order to switch between these two chord fingerings, almost every finger has to move to a different string or fret. This is too inefficient. Make it easier by playing the Em and G as shown in the following chord diagrams.

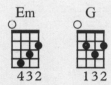

Notice how you can play a normal G chord and then just add your little finger to the 4th fret of the third string to play the Em chord. Since you only have to move one finger, this makes changing this chord a lot quicker.

Apply this same idea to other chords to eliminate the time it takes to change between chords. Just because there is a suggested finger position for a chord doesn't mean you should use that position in every situation. In a song, in order to make your chord changes smooth and quick with your strumming, experiment and try to find different ways to play chords that allow you to switch to the next chord faster.

'O Little Town of Bethlehem'

To put your chord vocabulary to the test, and to challenge your ability to switch between chords, 'O Little Town of Bethlehem' is a beautiful Christmas song with a lot of unique, yet pretty chord changes. Some of these chords might be new to you, so take time to introduce your fingers to these different positions in the next exercise.

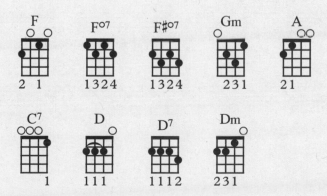

Because there is a lot of movement in the harmony and the melody of this song, it sounds good to strip back the strumming pattern to simple down strums. Sometimes the right strumming pattern is the one that is the most basic.

Track 72

O Little Town of Bethlehem

Chapter 6

Refining Advanced Strumming Techniques

- -

In This Chapter

▶ Exploring percussive strumming techniques

▶ Improving the touch strum and thumb 'n strum

▶ Learning four different rolling finger strums

- -

Chapters 4 and 5 show you how to practise a variety of different strumming patterns and techniques that can be applied to all sorts of songs. By now, you have a ton of ways of thinking about and dissecting the rhythm of a strumming pattern. So rather than focusing on just more patterns, in this chapter the attention turns to more advanced ways of strumming the ukulele.

In this chapter, discover how to strum percussively, develop rolling finger strums, and improve alternative strumming techniques like the touch strum and the thumb 'n strum. In addition, learn the strumming techniques and patterns that were used by musical greats like Israel Kamakawiwo'ole, Bob Marley, and James Brown.

Playing Percussively with Two Muting Techniques

Muting or dampening the strings while strumming makes a strumming pattern sound more rhythmic and percussive. You find percussive strumming in all sorts of musical styles like Hawaiian, reggae, funk, and even rock. There are two main ways to create a percussive strumming sound with your ukulele:

✔ Chnking

✔ Fret hand muting

Practise the following exercises at a variety of tempos to get used to using muted strums in all different types of musical situations.

Developing your 'chnking' technique

Use a *chnk* to add a percussive, clap-like, muted strum to any strumming pattern. To perform a chnk, strum down across the strings and immediately use the side or fleshy palm of your strumming hand to dampen the strings.

The chnk is a difficult movement to coordinate because it happens within a split second. If the chnk technique is new for you, or if you struggle with coordinating the movement, try practising it the following way:

1. **Take your strumming hand and lay the side of your palm across the strings just above the sound hole of the ukulele to dampen the strings.**

2. **While the side of your palm is in place dampening the strings, take your middle and ring fingers and practise flicking them across the strings of the ukulele. Try to angle your hand and fingers so the nail-side of your fingers is making the most contact with the strings to produce a nice scratchy *chnk* sound.**

Be mindful of any tension that collects in your body while practising this movement. You don't need to press into the strings very hard to dampen them and you don't have to dig into the strings very hard to get a nice chnk sound.

When you're ready, try making the chnk into one motion. Lift up your entire strumming hand a little bit off the strings. Proceed to perform a normal down strum on the ukulele with your middle and ring fingers, but as you go in for the strum, move your fingers across the strings while the side of your palm makes contact with the strings to dampen them.

To practise the chnk in a strumming pattern, take a regular down strum pattern and add a chnk strum to the second and fourth beats (represented by an *x*), as shown in the next exercise.

Track 73

Next, take a basic strumming pattern and practise chnking on the second and fourth beats, as shown in the next figure.

Track 74

To create a Hawaiian-style chnking strumming pattern, use a little bit of syncopation by removing the down strum on the third beat, as shown in this figure.

Track 75

Figuring out fret hand muting

Fret hand muting is another popular way to perform a muted strum. It produces a similar effect to the chnk, but instead of muting the strings with your strumming hand, mute the strings with your fretting hand.

Here's how to mute the strings with your fretting hand:

1. **Take your fretting hand and gently lay your fingers across the strings of the ukulele. Press down on the strings hard enough to prevent them from ringing out, but not too hard. The strings should not be pressed down to the fretboard.**

2. **Strum the strings of the ukulele like normal to perform a muted strum. Use more of the nail-side of your finger to produce a more percussive, 'scratchy' sound.**

If you do this right, none of the strings should ring out, and you should produce a nice crunchy muted sound.

In the next exercise, practise a fret hand mute on the second and fourth beats of the strumming pattern (muted beats are represented by an *x*).

Track 76

To improve your ability to switch your fretting hand between playing chords and muting the strings, use the fingers you aren't using to fret the chord to mute the strings, while keeping your other fingers in the position for the chord. In the case of the C chord in the above figure, the little finger works great for muting the strings since a lot of chord positions don't use it.

Here, only the down strums on the second and fourth beats are strummed to create a Bob Marley/Jason Mraz/reggae-style strumming feel.

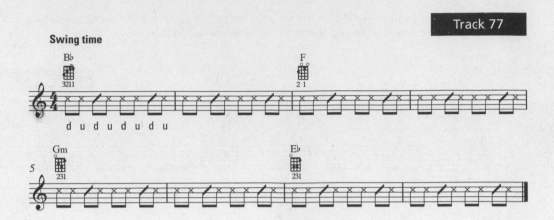

In this exercise, sixteenth note strums are used to create an energetic muted strumming pattern.

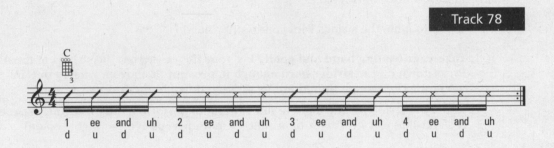

If you take the previous sixteenth note pattern, speed it up really fast, and accent other beats, you're able to create a funky James Brown strumming rhythm. In the next figure, the first and third beats in addition to the 'uh' of these beats are only played. The rest of the strums are muted. Take it slow at first.

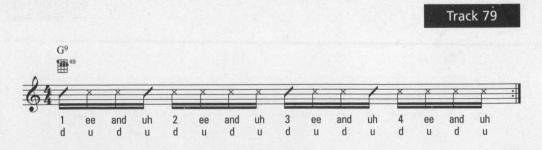

Play the G9 chord by barring the 4th fret with your index finger and using your middle finger to barre the bottom three strings on the 5th fret. Nine chords are very common in funk music.

'Michael, Row the Boat Ashore'

It's time to try out some muting in an actual song. In 'Michael, Row Your Boat Ashore' the second and fourth beats are accented using a muted strum. Either use a chnk or a fret hand mute for these beats.

Because a lot of modern music is centered around accenting the backbeat, for the vast majority of songs, accenting the second and fourth beats of a measure with a muted strum is a good way to go.

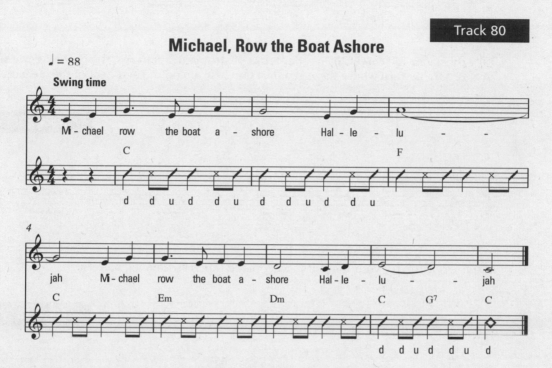

Track 80

Perfecting Alternative Strumming Techniques

Believe it or not, there are still some other ways to strum the ukulele to create even more interesting rhythms. Modern-day artists like Israel Kamakawiwo'ole (famous for his rendition of 'Somewhere Over the Rainbow'), Train ('Hey, Soul Sister'), and Jason Mraz ('I'm Yours') have been known to use these sorts of rhythms and ways of strumming in their music.

Taking on the touch strum

To perform a touch strum, in a down strum motion, lightly graze the top two strings of the ukulele. You might angle your strum away from the ukulele to avoid hitting the bottom two strings.

The next exercise shows one of the most common touch strum patterns. As the *t* indicates, the touch strums fall on beats one and three.

Track 81

Take this same idea and create other types of strumming patterns. the next exercise shows an alternate pattern where there is only a touch strum on the first beat of the measure.

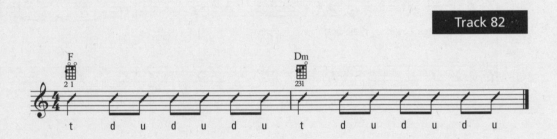

Track 82

In this exercise, try your hand at a syncopated touch strumming pattern.

Track 83

The touch strum works great in 3/4 time signatures too. In this exercise, add a touch strum to the first beat to give it that waltz feel.

Track 84

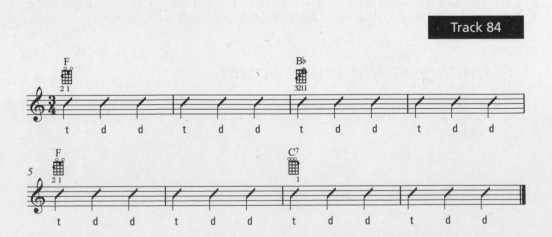

'Billy Boy'

Put your touch strum to work by playing the classic folk song 'Billy Boy'. Give the rhythm a nice pulse by swinging the beat and using a touch strum on beat one of the measure. This song is strummed at a pretty fast tempo, so be sure to start slow and build up speed from there.

Track 85

Billy Boy

Improving the thumb 'n strum

To use the thumb 'n strum in your playing, use your thumb to pluck the top string of the ukulele for the strong beats of the measure (beats 1 and 3) and strum like normal for the other beats.

The next figure shows a standard thumb 'n strum pattern. On the first and third beats, pluck the top string with your thumb. The thumb strums aren't meant to be the loudest strum, so there is no need to dig in as you pluck the string. Just imagine brushing or 'kissing' the top string.

Track 86

As you're strumming, keep your thumb hovering over the top string to always be ready to give it a nice pluck. For the regular down and up strums, strum less from the wrist and think more about lightly flicking your index finger over the strings. This prevents you from over-shooting the strings as you strum, so you can keep your thumb close to that top string.

Next, create a nice shuffle, country strum by alternating the plucking between the top two strings of the ukulele, as shown in the next figure. For this exercise, don't worry about only strumming the bottom three strings as you did in the previous exercise. For this pattern, strum through all four strings for the regular strums.

Track 87

 For every chord in the previous exercise, the first note that is plucked is the root note of the chord. For the G chord, a 'G' note is the root note of the chord, so you pluck the top G-string first. For a D chord, the 'D' note is plucked first on the second fret of the third string. For the C chord, the open C-string is plucked first. Plucking the root note of the chord first like this helps establish the overall sound of the chord to the listener's ears. To learn more about root notes, see Chapter 11.

In the next exercise, practise a reggae-style strumming pattern in the manner of Bob Marley. In a reggae strum, beats 1 and 3 often are missing to accent the backbeat. Use the thumb to pluck the 'and' of the first and third beat and strum a down and up strum to accent the second and fourth beats. This pattern sounds best played at a slow to medium tempo (60–88 BPM), if you have a metronome.

Track 88

To take the thumb 'n strum to another level, use your thumb to create waltzing melodies within your regular strumming pattern. Check out the next figure to play a waltz with passing notes inserted between chord changes.

Track 89

To reach the notes that fall on the 4th fret of the top string, use your little finger. This keeps your other fingers free to anticipate the next chord. For the last two measures of the exercise, slide up your little finger from the 4th to the 5th fret to play the last note.

Playing 'Rock a Bye Baby'

Put your skills to the test by playing the lullaby 'Rock a Bye Baby'. To play the song, use a 3/4 time signature thumb 'n strum pattern. As this song is a lullaby, don't forget to use a good sense of dynamics to play this song softly and tenderly.

Track 90

Rock a Bye Baby

Wrapping Your Mind Around Rolling Finger Strums

Mix up the simplest strumming pattern and impress your listeners with the rolling finger strum (often referred to as just a *roll strum* or *fan strum*). Roll strums are fast, quick strums that can be used to accent certain beats in a strumming pattern. You find the roll strum especially in flamenco and Hawaiian ukulele music.

Four finger roll

The *four finger roll* is one of the most basic ways to perform a roll strum. This way also tends to be more practical when it comes to implementing it into a strumming pattern. Use your little, ring, middle and index fingers, and perform the strum like so:

1. **With a loose hand, position your strumming hand so your four fingers are hovering over the strings above the sound hole and pointing towards the ground. You might have to tilt your wrist a little bit to get your fingers aimed for the ground.**

2. **While keeping the same hand position, bend your four fingers upwards into your hand. You're now ready to perform the four finger roll.**

3. **First, flick your little finger to strum down across the strings. Then, follow it up by flicking your ring finger down across the strings, then your middle finger, and finally, your index finger.**

The idea is to have the next finger strumming the strings just as the previous finger finishes strumming the strings. At first, it can be hard to get your fingers not to flick all at once. You're fingers will need a little bit of time to build up some independence from one another, so be sure to take it slow as you're starting. As you get better, speed it up so it's one quick, fluid motion.

Five finger roll

To perform the *five finger roll*, perform a four finger roll, but as soon as your index finger strums down across the last string, strum down again across the strings with the flesh side of your thumb. Because you're adding in the fifth finger, this makes the rolling strum sound even meatier.

There should be even space between each finger's strum. Ensure that there isn't a pause between when your index finger hits the last string and when your thumb strums through the strings. Modify the position of your thumb as needed to make the strum sound as even as possible.

Eight Finger Roll

For the *eight finger roll*, combine down strums and up strums. Use your little, ring, middle and index fingers to perform this roll strum like so:

1. **Like the four finger strum, position your strumming hand so your four fingers are hovering over the strings above the sound hole and pointing towards the ground. You're now ready to perform the eight finger roll.**

2. **For the first movements, you will be strumming *up* across the strings. First, strum your little finger up across the strings. Then, follow it by flicking your ringer up across the strings, then your middle finger, and lastly, your index finger.**

3. **Then, flick your little finger to strum *down* across the strings. Follow it up by flicking your ring finger to strum down across the strings, then your middle finger, and finally your index finger.**

When played in a fast, fluid motion, you're strumming the strings eight times in a split second! Because there is so much movement happening, it's *very* important you think about keeping your strumming hand and fingers as loose as possible. Roll strums sound the best when performed in a smooth, relaxed movement.

Ten Finger Roll

The mack daddy of all roll strums is the *ten finger roll*. It's like the eight finger roll, but add in the thumb like so:

1. **Strum up across the strings with the side of your thumb.**

2. **Follow that movement with consecutively flicking your little, ring, middle and index fingers up across the strings in that order.**

3. **Immediately following, flick your little, ring, middle, and index fingers down across the strings in that order.**

4. **Right after, complete the strum by strumming down across the strings with your thumb.**

The idea is that in the matter of a split second you are strumming the strings ten times! This is a tough strum to play cleanly, so if you don't get it at first, take a break and come back to it (that's to say, don't throw your ukulele across the room in a fit of frustration).

Practising finger roll strumming pattern exercises

The roll strum works best when used to accent certain beats of a strumming pattern. Just by using multiple fingers to perform a roll strum, you produce a good amount of volume to make a nice accent. In any case, the texture of a rolling strum sounds really cool, which makes it nice just for creating tonal variety in a strumming pattern.

In the next exercise, practise a roll strum on the first beat of the measure. The *R* stands for *rasgueado,* which is a term used in flamenco to refer to a roll strum. I recommend using the four finger roll in these exercises.

Track 91

Now, practise playing a roll strum on the second beat of the measure and immediately follow it up with an up strum, as shown in this exercise.

Track 92

Here, practise adding a roll strum to multiple beats of the measure.

Track 93

To create an even cooler rhythm, use a roll strum in combination with a chnk strum. In this exercise, the roll is placed on the first beat with the chnk on the second beat.

Track 94

Playing 'Sweet Lei Lehua'

'Sweet Lei Lehua' is a beautiful Hawaiian love song written by King David Kalakaua, the last king of Hawaii. It's a perfect song to practise adding in the roll strum. To really capture a Hawaiian feel, add the roll strum to the first beat of the strumming pattern and strum in swing time.

Sweet Lei Lehua

Part III
Becoming a Better Fingerpicker

Five Great Ways to Strengthen Your Fingerpicking Technique

- **Use alternation.** Alternation happens when you pluck consecutive notes on the same string with multiple fingers. Give it a try in your fingerpicking to increasing the speed and fluidity of single-note passages in an instrumental piece or solo.

- **Practise hammer-ons.** Learn how to move from a lower note to a higher while only plucking the string once. Press down your index finger, say, on the 1st fret of the bottom string, pluck the bottom string like normal, and while the string is still ringing, press down your middle finger on the 2nd fret of the bottom string.

- **Learn the art of the pull-off.** Get to grips with the pull-off, the opposite of the hammer-on. Move down from a higher note to a lower one with only one pluck of the string.

- **Slip slide away.** Use slides to add character to single-note passages, and string together multiple notes in a seamless way.

- **Combine strumming and fingerpicking for melody.** Taking a song that is normally sung and strummed, and turning it into an intricate fingerpicking arrangement puts an exciting new twist on the piece.

In this part . . .

- ✔ Pick your way through rhythmic fingerpicking.

- ✔ Learn the subtleties of fingerstyle.

- ✔ Fly solo with solo fingerpicking.

- ✔ Improve the speed, flexibility and fluidity of your picking.

- ✔ Strengthen your fingerpicking technique through engaging exercises.

- ✔ Go to `www.dummies.com/go/ukuleleexercises` to hear stylish fingerpicking on 'I Am a Poor Wayfaring Stranger' (Track 131; described in Chapter 8).

Chapter 7

Examining Fingerpicking Technique

••

In This Chapter

▶ Brushing up on fingerpicking technique

▶ Preparing your mind and body to fingerpick

••

*O*ne of the most beautiful ways to play the ukulele is by fingerpicking it. Fingerpicking on the ukulele can be divided up into two main styles: *rhythmic fingerpicking* and *fingerstyle*.

As the name would imply, rhythmic fingerpicking is a type of fingerpicking that provides a steady rhythm to a song, much like strumming, to allow you or others to sing the melody of the song. In this style of fingerpicking, you pick a pattern or sequence of notes that repeat over an entire song's chord progression. Fingerpicking in this way is a great way to add variety to a song you would normally strum. You might switch up a song by fingerpicking the song's chord progression rather than strumming it, or you can break up a song that you normally strum by fingerpicking certain sections and strumming others.

Fingerstyle, sometimes referred to as 'solo fingerpicking,' is a style of playing where you finger-pick the melody of a song without singing. Fingerstyle pieces can be famous, classical compositions or arrangements of popular songs you would normally sing. This style of fingerpicking is especially appealing if you don't see yourself as the strongest singer but still want to express the essence of a song through the ukulele without singing.

Each of these two fingerpicking styles use either of two popular fingerpicking techniques to pluck the strings of the ukulele with your fingers. In this chapter, you get started on the right foot by examining each fingerpicking technique and looking at the advantages and disadvantages of each, so you get the clearest sound from the ukulele.

Practising Two Different Fingerpicking Techniques

There are two main techniques used to fingerpick the ukulele. Of these two, one is not necessarily better than the other; you might find one of these techniques more beneficial to use over the other for certain songs. Be sure to practise each of these techniques because the patterns and pieces in the upcoming chapters make use of both.

Polishing the four-finger technique

The four-finger picking technique uses your thumb, index, middle, and ring fingers to pluck each of the strings. The thumb is assigned to pluck the top g-string of the ukulele, the index finger plucks the C-string, the middle finger plucks the E-string, and the ring finger plucks the A-string.

As for the little finger, some like to use it to press down gently on the top of the ukulele right below the sound hole. This can assist in stabilising your picking hand, which can help you more accurately pluck the strings. On the flip side, if you press too hard with your little finger, it creates tension in your hand that can slow your picking down. Proper picking technique dictates that you avoid using your little finger in this way. Just let it relax as you would every other finger to get the most speed and fluidity from your picking movement.

In music notation and ukulele tab, each finger used to pluck the strings is represented by the letters *p, i, m,* and *a.* These letters represent the Spanish word for each finger. The thumb (*pulgar*) is represented by *p*, the index finger (*indice*) is represented by *i*, the middle finger (*medio*) is represented by *m*, and the ring finger (*anular*) is represented by *a*. This method for identifying fingers originates from Spanish guitar pieces.

The following figure shows a basic fingerpicking pattern where you consecutively pluck each string using the four-finger technique. For now, don't worry about fretting a chord with your other hand and don't worry about keeping great timing, just pluck each string to get your fingers moving. Don't forget to keep your hand relaxed.

Track 96

The overall goal is to make each pluck as even sounding as possible in volume and in tone. This means, for example, that the string you pluck with your ring finger should be as loud as the string you pluck with your thumb. To ensure that each string rings out as clearly as the others, practise *planting* each finger in your picking hand.

When you plant a finger, you rest the tip of your finger on the string before plucking it. By doing this, you ensure that you make the fullest contact with your finger on the string. The better the contact you make with a string, the richer the tone will be, and your picking becomes more accurate.

To practise planting, take the previous fingerpicking pattern that uses the four-finger technique. First, plant, or rest, the tip of your thumb on the top g-string. Then, pluck the top string with your thumb, but as you are plucking the string, move the tip of your index finger to plant on the C-string. Pluck the C-string with your index finger, and as you do that, plant the tip of your middle finger on the E-string. Proceed to pluck the E-string with your middle finger while planting the tip of your ring finger on the bottom A-string. Lastly, pluck the A-string with your ring finger.

You should think of the plucking and planting as one motion. While you're plucking a string, the next finger used in the pattern should be planting as the string is being plucked. Check out the following figure to see this process broken down. Play the pattern slow at first and think about exaggerating the plucking and planting movements. This allows you to get the feeling for making contact with the strings. As you get more comfortable, gradually speed up the motion, so the space between plucking and planting becomes less noticeable and more fluid.

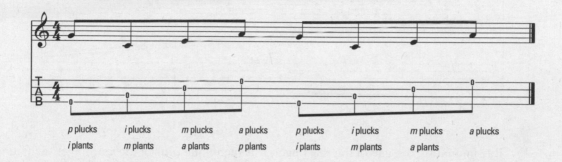

| p plucks | i plucks | m plucks | a plucks | p plucks | i plucks | m plucks | a plucks |
| i plants | m plants | a plants | p plants | i plants | m plants | a plants | |

When you practise planting at a slow tempo, you inevitably mute the strings, which produces a slightly uneven sound. This is okay as you practise, because you are using the planting exercise to get the feeling for plucking the strings with your fingers. As you get comfortable and speed up, the feeling becomes smoother and more seamless. Because the ukulele is a smaller instrument than a guitar or piano, each string doesn't sustain volume for as long as their strings do, because both have bigger chambers for resonating the sound. Aside from the previous planting exercise, for the fingerpicking patterns and exercises in this book in general, let the strings ring out as long as possible before plucking them again to produce the richest tone.

You don't need very long nails to fingerpick. A lot of people just use the fleshy part of the tips of their fingers. This produces a warmer, softer sound than using your nails. If you choose to pluck the strings with your nails, the tone becomes brighter and grittier. To get a blend between both sounds, aim to attack the strings at the part of your finger between the nail and fleshy part of the fingertip. Each way produces a different tone from the ukulele. Experiment to see what sounds best to your ears.

The four-finger picking technique works well for rhythmic fingerpicking patterns (such as the ones in Chapter 8) since each string is assigned a different finger. The biggest reason why you might not choose the four-finger technique is because the ring finger tends to be your weakest finger. If you're new to fingerpicking, it takes practice and exercise to get this finger to act as strongly as the other fingers, but you can easily overcome the weakness, especially with the arpeggio exercises in Chapter 9.

Perfecting the alternating thumb technique

In the alternating thumb technique, you use your thumb, index, and middle fingers to pluck the strings of the ukulele. The thumb alternates between plucking the top two strings of the ukulele: the g-string and C-string. The index finger is assigned to pluck the E-string, and the middle finger is assigned to pluck the bottom A-string.

Take a look at the following figure to see a basic fingerpicking pattern that uses the alternating thumb technique. For now, don't worry about playing any particular chord, just focus on plucking each of the open strings with your fingers. In addition, for this pattern, don't forget to plant your fingers like you did for the four-finger technique.

By eliminating the use of the ring finger, this technique (unlike the four-finger technique) is appealing because you use your three strongest fingers to fingerpick. In addition, the thumb is assigned to pluck the lowest pitched string of the ukulele, which happens to be the third string: the C-string. To some people, using your thumb to pluck the lowest-pitched string can feel more intuitive, especially if you come from a guitar background.

At the same time, using the alternating thumb technique causes your thumb to get a little bit more of a workout. This technique is nice to use for solo fingerpicking pieces, where a lot of the focus in the piece is playing notes on the bottom two strings of the ukulele with your index and middle fingers (such as the pieces in Chapters 9 and 10).

Looking at the Golden Rules of Fingerpicking

As with the golden rules of strumming in Chapter 3, when it comes to fingerpicking on the ukulele, there are a couple key things to keep in mind as you move into practising the fingerpicking exercises and pieces of music in the pages to come. By examining these rules, you help focus your fingerpicking practice and ultimately improve your technique.

Rule #1: Stay loose

Whenever you learn a new fingerpicking pattern, it takes time for your fingers to get the hang of it, even if you've been fingerpicking for awhile. In an attempt to get your fingers to pluck the right strings at the right moment, you might, without even realising it, tense up your picking hand and fingers. Unfortunately, in the long run, this tension slows you down, hinders the clarity of notes, and can cause your picking hand to cramp up and experience soreness.

Fingerpicking, when done correctly, should feel light and easy. To create sound from the strings, it doesn't require a lot of contact from the tips of your fingers. As you practise, be sure to monitor any tension in your hand. Tension can stem from poor posture, forgetting to breathe, and forgetting to warm up (Chapter 1 addresses these items). If you do experience any pain or soreness while fingerpicking, don't worry about it; take a break and come back to picking at a later time.

Rule #2: Slow and steady wins the race

Like strumming, fingerpicking the ukulele is all about keeping a steady sense of rhythm. However, in an attempt to keep your fingerpicking steady, it's important that you don't tense up. For the most part, it's easier to stay relaxed when you take it slow. However, what happens when you want to speed it up? There are a couple ways to keep a relaxed, steady rhythm while getting faster.

Considering the use of the metronome

Unlike strumming, right off the bat, I don't recommend using a metronome while you're learning new fingerpicking patterns, arpeggios, or pieces of music. Sometimes the pressure of keeping steady time with a metronome can create tension throughout your wrist and the fingers of your picking hand. Staying loose and avoiding tension while picking is crucial. If you have a metronome, first get your fingers used to the movement of whatever fingerpicking pattern you are learning, and then, once you are comfortable, work on making your fingerpicking steadier by incorporating the use of the metronome to practise at a variety of tempos.

Fingerpicking at blazing fast speeds

Before you can play fast, you have to put in the work of playing slow. That is to say, if you can't pluck the strings accurately and smoothly at a slow tempo, it's likely you will repeat the same mistakes when you speed up the tempo. In this way, as you practise fingerpicking slowly, try to make it the best you can in terms of steadiness and consistency of rhythm, tone, and volume, so when it comes time to bump up the tempo, you can more easily transition into faster speeds. To practise in this way, if you have a metronome, set it at a slow tempo (60–84 BPM) while you practise a fingerpicking pattern. As you get comfortable at this slower speed, bump your metronome up in 5–10 BPM increments to increase your fingerpicking speed.

Though a metronome can be a useful practice tool for improving fingerpicking speed, as I mentioned before, you shouldn't always use it. One of the best ways to improve fingerpicking speed is to practise certain patterns or sections of a solo fingerpicking piece in quick bursts of speed for short periods of time. Then, gradually extend those bursts of speed to longer periods of time. Not only does fingerpicking fast require looseness in your picking hand, it also requires a degree of endurance and strength to maintain that level of movement and speed. By practising in shorter bursts of speed, you get used to the feeling of fingerpicking fast without completely exhausting your picking hand. Over time, as you increase your endurance, you will be able to maintain steadiness and consistency at a fast speed while feeling less fatigued.

Rule #3: Repeat, repeat, repeat

Fingerpicking is a lot like learning your first couple of chords on the ukulele. If you recall, it took a while for the fingers of your fretting hand to get used to the correct position of those chords. However, as you practised those chord positions over and over again, it got easier. Likewise, with your picking hand, it takes your fingers time to get used to all the different picking movements that might be required from a fingerpicking pattern or a piece of music.

Because of this, you need to play practice pieces repetitively to improve your fingerpicking technique. As you practise a pattern or a passage of music over and over, you build those movements into your muscle memory, so your fingers automatically know where to go without much conscious effort. To get to that point, you have to be willing to put in the time.

More than that though, you have to be willing to break down a fingerpicking pattern or a passage of music into small parts. Rather than tackling an entire pattern, you might focus on using your fingers to pluck the first two notes of the pattern over and over again. As that motion becomes comfortable, add in the next note of the pattern, and so on. Similarly, for a solo fingerpicking piece, you might just focus on learning the first couple measures of the piece, and then, when you have those mastered, move on to the next few measures. Diligently practising like this is extremely rewarding, because there comes that point where everything clicks and your fingers 'get it.'

Another word for repetition is *practice*. If you're not seeing the progress as fast you'd like for a particular fingerpicking pattern, be patient with yourself and keep at it. Don't give up on one pattern to move to another out of frustration. Stay focused and only select a couple patterns to work through and master at a time. With consistent practice and dedication, you are bound to see improvement.

There is a saying, 'No pain, no gain.' This is not an idea you want to subscribe to when it comes to fingerpicking. It's possible to experience a little soreness after a practice session, but you should never practise or repeat a pattern or passage of music to the point of pain, or where your picking hand is rendered useless. Be sure to take frequent breaks to rest your hands and your mind.

Chapter 8

Developing Rhythmic Fingerpicking Patterns

In This Chapter

▶ Making your picking clear and rock-steady

▶ Learning multi-purpose rhythmic fingerpicking patterns

▶ Taking fingerpicking patterns and playing actual songs

*I*n this chapter, you become well versed in the style of rhythmic fingerpicking on the ukulele. This style of fingerpicking requires you to pluck a pattern of notes that repeats over a song's chord progression. This provides a steady and consistent rhythmic foundation for a song, which allows you or someone else to sing out the melody of the song as you fingerpick. Practise the rhythmic fingerpicking pattern exercises in this chapter to play all sorts of songs on the ukulele.

This chapter focuses on two techniques used in the rhythmic fingerpicking style: four-finger picking technique and alternating picking technique. As Chapter 7 makes clear, both of these techniques have different advantages and disadvantages. Most of it comes down to personal taste, but I recommend practising both to ensure you're ready in any given situation.

From this chapter, select only a few pattern exercises to work on at a time. To stay focused, keep track of your progress in your practice journal by writing down the exercises you are working on. Don't overwhelm yourself by trying to tackle every exercise in this chapter at once. For each pattern in this chapter, take time to learn it by practising over just one chord. First, play the pattern at a slow tempo (60–84 BPM, if you have a metronome) and count out loud as you practise to try to get your fingers moving at a steady and consistent rhythm. Then, as you feel more comfortable with the pattern, introduce a chord change or two. In time, bump up the tempo gradually to increase your fingerpicking speed. When you get even more comfortable, try your hand at coming up with your very own fingerpicking patterns!

Practising the Four-Finger Picking Technique

The following rhythmic fingerpicking exercises explore patterns that use the four-finger picking technique, as discussed in Chapter 7. This means using your thumb (represented by a *p*) to pluck the top string, index finger (represented by an *i*) to pluck the third string, middle finger (represented by an *m*) to pluck the second string, and ring finger (represented by an *a*) to pluck the bottom string.

For each of these patterns, as you pluck each string, let the string ring out as long as possible before plucking it again.

'Inside-out' pattern

As the name implies, the 'inside-out' pattern starts by plucking each of the middle two strings and then plucking each of the outside strings, as shown in the following figure.

Track 98

Focus on making each string ring out as clearly as possible at the same volume and intensity. Keep the rhythm as steady as you can. Take it slow at first.

Watch out for tension in your hand, wrist, and fingers. You don't need to pluck the strings very hard to make them ring out. If you notice your hand cramping up, take a break and stretch your fingers, then come back to it.

When you are able to play the 'inside-out' pattern at a steady, consistent tempo, add in a chord change, as shown in the following exercise.

Track 99

Use the 'inside-out' pattern to practise switching between other chords as shown in the following figure. Once you get this down, experiment using the 'inside-out' pattern with other chord progressions that you come up with on your own.

Track 100

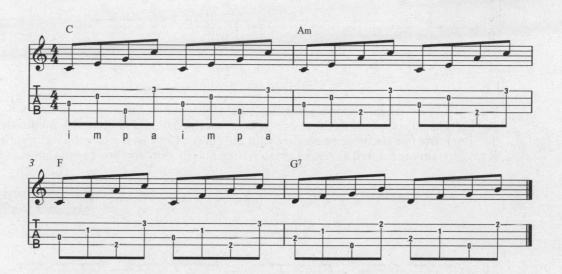

Please note that the Am chord in the second measure and the F chord in the third measure of the figure above is fretted slightly different than it's been presented in other chord diagrams throughout the book. In this position of the Am chord, place your middle finger on the 2nd fret of the fourth string and your little finger on the 3rd fret of the first string. In this position of the F chord, place your index finger on the 1st fret of the second string, middle finger on the 2nd fret of the fourth string, and little finger on the 3rd fret of the first string. Although these finger positions are different, they are still an Am and F chord because all of the notes that make up an Am chord (A-C-E) and F chord (F-A-C) are still being played. The notes are just arranged in a different order. In fingerpicking, it's common to play chords in different positions across the fretboard to get a different sound. Check out Chapter 13 to learn more about playing chords in new, varied ways.

Fingerpicking is quite the juggling act; you're required to make your fingers perform completely separate movements. Be patient with yourself and take things slowly. Keep at it because fingerpicking is all about repetition; the more you do it the more it becomes second nature – to the point where, believe it or not, you don't have to think much about it!

'Outside-in' pattern

Coming up with creative fingerpicking patterns is largely about changing the order of how you pluck the strings. In the 'outside-in' pattern, flip the 'inside-out' pattern on its head by plucking each of the outside strings first and then plucking each of the inside strings, as shown in the following figure. This gives a different sound to the same chords because you're plucking the notes of the chord in a different order.

Track 101

Next, practise changing chords using the 'outside-in' pattern. Take adequate time before playing this exercise to practise changing between the different chords without fingerpicking. The more familiar your fingers are with the chords the easier it is to keep the entire fingerpicking uninterrupted as you change chords. Take it slow and don't rush things.

Track 102

It's not uncommon in an actual song to vary a fingerpicking pattern throughout different sections, such as a verse or a chorus, to create interest for your listener. In the following exercise, for the first measure, use the 'inside-out' pattern; then, for the last measure, use the 'outside-in' pattern.

Track 103

Simultaneous pinched patterns

To perform a *pinch*, pluck multiple notes at the same time within a fingerpicking pattern. This makes a picking pattern sound more complex and intricate. In the following exercise, simultaneously pluck the top and bottom string with your thumb and ring finger on the first and third beats of the measure.

Track 104

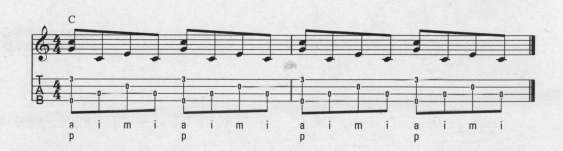

Take this same simultaneous fingerpicking pattern and use it over a common chord progression, as shown in the next figure.

Track 105

Use a little bit of creativity and pinch together other strings in the pattern to come up with a completely different sound. In the following exercise, simultaneously pluck the middle two strings with your index and ring fingers for the first and third beats of the measure.

Track 106

Make a fingerpicking pattern sound more complex by varying between pinching the outside strings and middle two strings, as shown in the following exercise. In a song, you might decide to vary a pattern like this, because when you pinch together different notes of a chord, it creates a different sound and texture to the overall pattern, which might be desirable.

Track 107

The next four fingerpicking patterns explore different ways to incorporate the pinch into your fingerpicking. Practise these and even try coming up with your own patterns.

Track 108

Track 109

Track 110

Track 111

 Part of becoming a proficient fingerpicker is being able to navigate between different chords. As you did for the earlier exercises, practise the previous simultaneous fingerpicking patterns over different chord changes by using the chord progressions in previous exercises, or come up with your own.

Patterns in varied rhythms

So far, the fingerpicking patterns have been evenly divided up; meaning, each pluck in the pattern is held for the same amount of time. The following exercises look at the use of different rhythms and timings to make a fingerpicking pattern sound even more complex and interesting.

In this first exercise, hold out the first and third beats for a quarter note and pluck eighth notes on the second and fourth beats. This means the plucks on the first and third beats are held twice as long as the other plucks. Pay attention to the numbers below the pattern so you can count out loud as you practise.

Track 112

Create a whole different feel to a fingerpicking pattern by not plucking the strings on certain beats. In the following figure, you pluck the bottom string on the 'and' of the second beat and hold it through the third beat, then pluck the second string on the 'and' of the third beat. This creates a *syncopated* fingerpicking pattern because you aren't plucking a string on the third beat of the measure. Take a look at the following figure to see what this looks like, and see Chapter 4 to learn more about different types of syncopation.

Track 113

Fingerpicking patterns can also be played in a shuffle rhythm (see Chapter 5 for an in-depth look at shuffle rhythm). In a shuffle rhythm (sometimes referred to as *swing time*), plucks that fall on the main beats of the measure (beats 1, 2, 3, or 4) are held twice as long as plucks that fall on the 'and' of the beat. A pattern played in a shuffle rhythm is normally indicated by the words 'Swing time' at the beginning of the music. In the following exercise, take a regular 'inside-out' pattern and switch between playing in a straight and in a shuffle rhythm. Be sure to listen to the audio to hear how this sounds.

Track 114

The blues are famous for using shuffle rhythms. Use an 'inside-out' pattern in swing time to fingerpick the 12-bar blues in the following figure. All of the chords in the 12-bar blues change on the first beat of the measure except for the G7 chord that changes on the third beat in measure 12.

Track 115

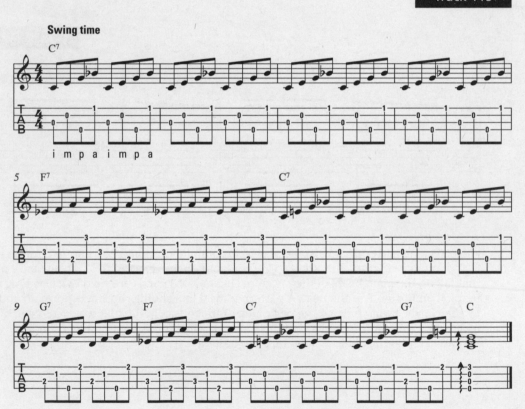

So far, all the fingerpicking patterns you've seen have been in 4/4 time signature, where there are four counts per measure. The following two patterns are played in 3/4 time signature, so you are counting three beats per measure. Count out loud as you practise these.

Track 116

Track 117

Playing 'The Water Is Wide'

Take any of the fingerpicking patterns you've learned so far and use them to play and sing a song. Because the patterns in this chapter are steady and consistent, they are best used to provide the underlying rhythm of a song as you or someone else sings the melody of the song. In fact, you might take the songs you strummed in Part II of this book 'Becoming a Better Strummer' and apply a fingerpicking pattern you learned in this chapter to play and sing the song.

'The Water Is Wide' uses a simple pinch pattern throughout the entire song. Before looking at the fingerpicking pattern, check out the following figure to see what chords are used in this song. The more comfortable you are with the chord positions the easier it will be to keep your fingerpicking as steady and consistent as possible throughout the song. Notice that the Am chord is played slightly different than a 'normal' Am chord.

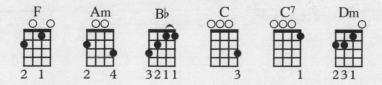

Next, take a look at the music and tab for 'The Water Is Wide'. As you start to learn this song, don't worry about singing. First, practise the fingerpicking pattern shown in the first couple measures over an F chord. When you are comfortable playing the pattern over a single chord, take the song in four bar sections. For example, in the first four measures, just practise switching between an F chord and a Bb chord. As you practise, be sure to count out loud. Almost all of the chord changes happen on beat one of the measure, but notice that in measures 3 and 13, there is a chord change on the third beat. Take it slow at first and only try to sing the song when you are able to play through the song's form with the pattern and chord changes in a steady, consistent rhythm.

Track 118

The Water Is Wide

Practising the Alternating Picking Technique

Now, take a look at fingerpicking patterns that use the alternating picking technique. In the alternating picking technique, your thumb (represented by a *p*) is used to alternate between plucking the top two strings of the ukulele. Assign your index finger (represented by an *i*) to pluck the second string and your middle finger (represented by an *m*) to pluck the bottom string. Check out Chapter 7 for an in-depth look at this technique.

Throughout these pattern exercises, try to make the overall sound of the pattern as consistent and even as possible. This means all the plucks in the pattern should be around the same volume and tone. In addition, monitor any tension that creeps up in your picking hand. If you start to get sore, stop, take a break, and stretch your fingers. Then, come back to it at a slow tempo. Don't rush things. Take time to get it right.

'Inside-out' pattern

Like the four-finger picking technique, you're able to play the 'inside-out' fingerpicking pattern using the alternating picking technique, as shown in the following chord progression.

Track 119

'Outside-in' pattern

Practise an 'outside-in' fingerpicking pattern using the alternating picking technique.

Track 120

Take one chord and practise switching between the 'inside-out' and 'outside-in' pattern using the alternating picking technique, as shown in the following figure.

Track 121

Simultaneous pinched patterns

The following patterns incorporate a pinch, where you pluck two notes at the same time using the alternating picking technique.

Track 122

Track 123

Track 124

Track 125

Practise each of these patterns over different chord progressions so you're able to use these patterns in any song. Use chord progressions in previous exercises or write out your own.

Patterns in varied rhythms

Break up a fingerpicking pattern by holding certain notes longer than others. In this exercise, hold the first and third beats for a quarter note in length, and for the second and fourth beats, play eighth notes. Count this out loud to sense where these plucks fall within the pattern.

Track 126

In the next figure, use an 'outside-in' fingerpicking pattern, but don't pluck the third beat of the measure. This creates a syncopated fingerpicking pattern that has a completely different feel than a normal 'outside-in' pattern.

Track 127

A great exercise is to go through the fingerpicking patterns you've learned so far and apply a shuffle rhythm, which feels lazy and laidback. To practise this, set your metronome and switch between playing a straight, normal rhythm and a shuffle rhythm. In the following figure, the first measure of the exercise is played in normal, straight time, and then, the second measure switches to swing time. Check out the audio to hear the difference.

Track 128

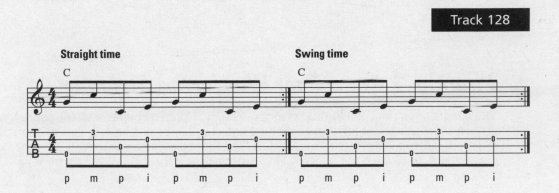

The next two figures show fingerpicking patterns using the alternating picking technique in 3/4 time signature.

Track 129

Track 130

Playing 'I Am a Poor Wayfaring Stranger'

The song 'I Am a Poor Wayfaring Stranger' centres around a couple of minor chords, which gives it a sad-but-beautiful, darker sound. First, check out the following figure to practise the different chord positions used in this song. The more familiar you are with the chords the easier it will be to keep the fingerpicking pattern steady throughout the entire song.

Next, take a look at the music and tab for 'I Am a Poor Wayfaring Stranger.' The fingerpicking pattern is a simple, alternating pattern in swing time that repeats itself throughout the entire song. At first, just practise the fingerpicking pattern over a Dm chord. When you're able to play the pattern at a steady tempo, practise playing through the song's chord changes without singing. Once you're able to do that, practise humming the melody, and eventually, singing out the melody.

Track 131

I'm Just a Poor Wayfaring Stranger

Chapter 9

Improving Your Solo Fingerpicking Skills

In This Chapter

▶ Increasing fingerpicking speed and accuracy with arpeggio exercises

▶ Using tremolo technique to create intricate fingerpicking melodies

▶ Performing solo fingerpicking pieces on ukulele

*I*n this chapter, you dive right into the world of solo fingerpicking on the ukulele, also known as *fingerstyle*. You learn how to play several different pieces from world famous composers like Matteo Carcassi (1792–1853), Dionisio Aguado (1784–1849), and Francisco Tárrega (1852–1909). Many of these pieces were originally written for the guitar in the Classical and Romantic music periods, but they sound just as beautiful when performed on the ukulele.

The great thing about composers like Carcassi, Aguado and Táregga is that a large part of their repertoire included short pieces called *études* (a French word for 'study') that focus on specific aspects of fingerpicking technique. This means you become a better fingerpicker while making actual, beautiful-sounding music. Not only do these pieces help your technique but they are also some of the most rewarding to play on the ukulele.

In this chapter, you learn how to play a handful of different études. In addition, you discover various arpeggio exercises that help improve the movement, clarity and speed in your fingerpicking hand. Not only do these exercises get your fingers moving but these arpeggios are often used in fingerstyle pieces to create an elaborate, graceful sound. Along with arpeggios, you try your hand at two tremolo techniques that produce a fast, shimmering sound from the ukulele.

 For your benefit, there are *a lot* of exercises in this chapter. To get the most out of these exercises, it's best to select a few to practise at a time. This way you don't overwhelm yourself.

Tackling Solo Fingerstyle Pieces

Approaching a solo piece of music on the ukulele is a little different than learning a rhythmic fingerpicking pattern that repeats itself over an entire song (such as the patterns in Chapter 8). For fingerstyle pieces, your fingers are often required to navigate between different positions and different strings. To start off, practise a couple of beginning fingerstyle arrangements. The following songs are perfect for getting your fingers in the mode to play more intricate pieces in the pages to come.

Take it slow. Fingerstyle pieces often take longer to learn than a song where you'd just strum the chords. This is normal. Break up the song into sections and give your fingers time to get used to the different movements. By doing this, you can enjoy the process of becoming a better fingerpicker while having fun!

Learning two pieces of music

To start off, learn how to fingerpick a solo arrangement of 'Twinkle, Twinkle Little Star'. This song gets your fingers used to plucking single-note melodies and multiple notes at once. Use your thumb (represented by a *p*) to pluck the top string, index finger (represented by an *i*) to pluck the third string and middle finger (represented by an *m*) to pluck the second string.

Track 132

Twinkle, Twinkle Little Star

Next, take a look at the following arrangement of 'Yankee Doodle'. You play this piece on the bottom three strings using your index, middle and ring finger (represented by an *a*). Notice how in measure 6, little numbers are printed next to the notes on the music staff. These numbers provide a suggested fingering for your fretting hand, with the number 1 indicating your index finger, number 2 indicating your middle finger, number 3 indicating your ring finger and number 4 indicating your little finger. In this case, position your index, middle and ring fingers in the suggested way to more easily switch between the notes.

Yankee Doodle

Track 133

 For both of these pieces, think about making each pluck as even and consistent sounding as possible. For example, notes plucked with your thumb should be just as loud as notes plucked with your ring finger. If you notice that certain notes aren't ringing out as loud as they could be, think about giving the pluck a little bit more effort.

Playing Carcassi's 'Andantino'

Carcassi's 'Andantino' is the second work in his Opus 59. In this piece, notes are played on all four strings of the ukulele. This piece is an excellent exercise in challenging your fingers to pluck multiple notes at the same time with different finger combinations. Use the four-finger picking technique for this song where your thumb, index, middle and ring fingers are assigned to pluck each string (see Chapter 7 for more on fingerpicking techniques).

The Italian word *andantino* refers to a piece of music that is played lightheartedly and quickly. Before trying to play this piece too quickly, first work on playing it at a slower, consistent tempo; then, gradually speed it up.

 The most challenging aspect to this piece is switching between the notes quickly enough in measure 7. To set yourself up to play this measure smoothly, fret the notes in measures 5 and 6 with your middle and little fingers as indicated in the music to free up your index finger. Then, in measure 7, take your index finger and perform a *barre* at the 7th fret, which means you take your index finger and lay it across and press down all four strings at the 7th fret. Be sure to check out the numbers next to the notes in the music to get an idea for the fingering through this section.

Track 134

Andantino, Op. 59 no. 2

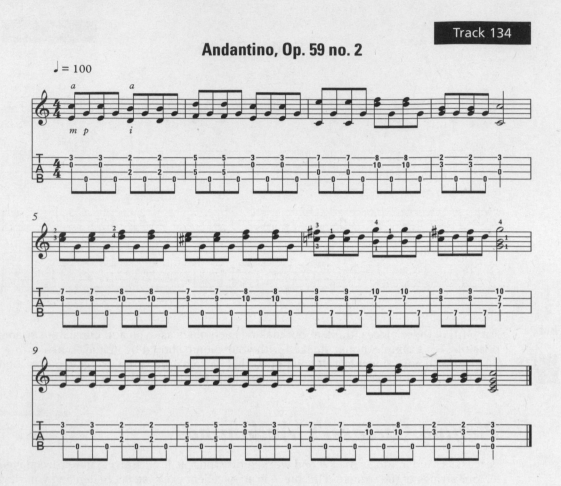

Strengthening Your Fingerpicking with Arpeggio Exercises

An *arpeggio* is a chord where you pluck the notes of the chord individually with your picking hand. Practising arpeggios is beneficial for many reasons. For one, arpeggios make excellent warm-up exercises because they get your fingers moving in various ways. In addition, they help build speed, strength, accuracy and finger independence in your picking hand, which is essential for playing an intricate fingerstyle piece or a rock-steady fingerpicking pattern for a song. Lastly, some of the most famous fingerstyle pieces ever composed are based around arpeggios.

Each of the following arpeggio exercises target the use of certain fingers in your picking hand. For each exercise, at first, play through the pattern slowly to get a feel for the movement of your fingers across the strings. Listen to how each of your fingers are connecting with the strings and focus on producing the same amount of volume from each finger. Try to make the arpeggio sound as even, steady and consistent as possible. To create the fullest sound, be sure to let each string ring out as long as possible before plucking it again. Vary between playing these arpeggios at slow and fast speeds.

For each arpeggio, at first, don't worry about using a metronome. Just get a feel for the pattern. Sometimes the pressure of keeping good timing with the metronome can create tension. Once you're able to play through the pattern in a relaxed way, add in the use of a metronome if you have one to tighten up your timing and rhythm.

Trying your hand at 'p i m' arpeggios

This first group of arpeggio exercises uses your thumb (represented by a *p*), index finger (represented by an *i*), and middle finger (represented by an *m*). Each exercise changes between a C and G7 chord. Additionally, each arpeggio pattern is presented in three different ways: 1) on the bottom three strings, 2) on the top three strings, and 3) a gapped version where the thumb plucks the top string and the index and middle fingers pluck the bottom two strings.

Since these arpeggios are groups of three notes, play these patterns in eighth note triplets counting: *1 - trip - let*, *2 - trip - let*, etc.

'P i m' arpeggio variations

Track 135

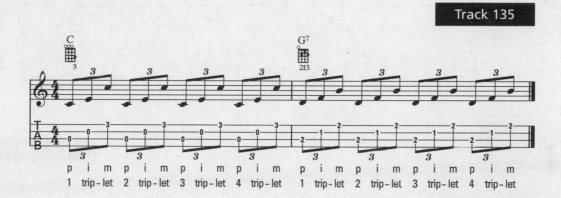

Track 136

Track 137

'I m p' arpeggio variations

Track 138

Track 139

Track 140

'M p i' arpeggio variations

Track 141

Track 142

Track 143

'M i p' arpeggio variations

Track 144

Track 145

m i p

Track 146

m i p

In the next group of *p i m* exercises, take the previous arpeggios and alternate your thumb between the top two strings. Assign your index finger to pluck the second string and middle finger to pluck the bottom string. These patterns not only challenge your fingers, but they also start to sound more intricate and melodic.

Alternating thumb 'p i m' arpeggio and variations

Track 147

p i m

Playing Tárrega's 'Étude in E minor'

Tárrega's 'Étude in E minor' is a perfect example of using arpeggios in a melodic, complex-sounding way. Although the fingerpicking sounds complex, in reality this song is a standard *m i p* arpeggio like the ones you practised in the previous group of arpeggio exercises. This means, once you know how to play the arpeggio, it's just a matter of figuring out how to fret the different notes with your other hand.

The trickiest chord position shows up in measures 3, 7 and 15. To play this position, use your index finger to barre the bottom three strings at the 2nd fret. Then, position your ring finger on the 4th fret of the second string. While maintaining this position, you're able to alter the chord throughout the measure using your little and middle finger as indicated by the fingering numbers. Likewise, apply this same idea in measure 10 to barre the bottom three strings on the 5th fret with your index finger.

Lastly, check out measures 8 and 16. For these measures, pluck the C-string and A-string with your thumb and middle finger. While these strings are ringing out, position your index finger at the 12th fret to barre the bottom two strings. Strum or pluck these two strings.

'Étude in E minor' is originally written for guitar, so when this piece is played on the guitar, it sounds in the key of E minor. Because this piece is arranged for ukulele, it sounds in A minor, since the ukulele is tuned differently to a guitar.

Track 151

Étude in E minor

Compose your very own étude by coming up with your own chord progressions, especially using moveable chord shapes (see Chapter 13). Then, select an arpeggio that you learned in the previous exercises to fingerpick the chords.

Working through more advanced arpeggios

For these next exercises, add in the use of your ring finger (represented by an *a*). You might find that some of these arpeggios are awkward and feel more comfortable to play without the use of your ring finger, but the point of these exercises isn't to find the path of least resistance; the goal is to work out and strengthen your ring finger by focusing on its use through these patterns.

The strings that are plucked with the ring finger should be as loud as the strings plucked with other fingers. Because the ring finger tends to be the weakest of the fingers, think about giving a bit more effort when plucking with this finger.

In the first four exercises, assign your thumb to pluck the top string, index finger to the third string, middle finger to second string and ring finger to the bottom string.

Track 152

Track 153

Track 154

Track 155

The next four exercises remove the use of the thumb and focus on working out the index, middle and ring fingers on the bottom three strings.

Track 156

Track 157

Track 158

Track 159

The following arpeggio exercises use your thumb, index, middle, or ring fingers. Unlike the previous arpeggio exercises, these are written in a four-note arpeggio pattern. Count the exercises in sixteenth notes, as shown in the following figure.

Track 160

Track 161

Track 162

Track 163

Playing Aguado's '25 Piéces Pour Guitare, no. 17'

The following piece is adapted to ukulele from Aguado's *25 Piéces Pour Guitare* – a collection of guitar studies. The piece features a constant *i m a* arpeggio with frequent changes in the fretting hand. Not only do the chords in this piece create a rich, beautiful sound, but the piece provides a nice workout for your picking and fretting hand.

To make transitions between notes smoother, remember to 'set up' chord changes. For example, in the first two groups of triplets in measure 3, use your index finger to fret the 1st fret of the second string and middle finger to fret the 2nd fret of the third string. While you're picking through this chord, hover your ring finger over the 3rd fret of the second string to prepare to play the second two sets of triplets in the measure.

You could play this song using a *p i m* arpeggio but the main goal in learning this piece is to exercise the use of your ring finger. Although it's tempting to avoid using your ring finger, because it tends to be the weakest, you have a lot more flexibility and options when it comes to playing more complicated fingerstyle pieces if you're able to use your ring finger as equally well as your other fingers.

Track 164

25 Piéces Pour Guitare, no. 17

Developing Lightning-Fast Tremolo Technique

Tremolo is a fast fingerpicking technique that plucks a certain string multiple times (usually the bottom string) to produce a shimmery, glistening sound. It's a common classical and flamenco guitar technique, but it sounds particularly well when used on the ukulele. You can hear this technique in modern-day ukulele player Jake Shimabukuro's arrangement of Franz Schubert's 'Ave Maria'.

Tackling three-finger tremolo

The three-finger tremolo uses your thumb, index and middle fingers. The index and middle fingers exclusively alternate between plucking the bottom string starting with the middle finger first. The thumb alternates between plucking the top three strings. For this first exercise, assign your thumb to pluck the second string.

Track 165

There should be no difference in volume between plucking the bottom string with your index finger or middle finger. Go slow at first and focus on making both of these fingers sound as even as possible as they alternate to pluck the bottom string. At the same time, don't forget to relax and breathe through the exercise to avoid cramping up.

In the next exercise, take it a step further and practise alternating your thumb between the top three strings to create an arpeggiated melody in addition to the tremolo.

Track 166

Playing 'Étude in C major'

The three-finger tremolo can be difficult at first, but as you practise the technique over time, you build it into your muscle memory, which means you'll be able to think less and less about the movement of your fingers. As your fingers get more comfortable, speed the tremolo up and add in other chord changes to create beautiful and delicate sounding harmonies and melodies, as shown in the following 'Étude in C major'.

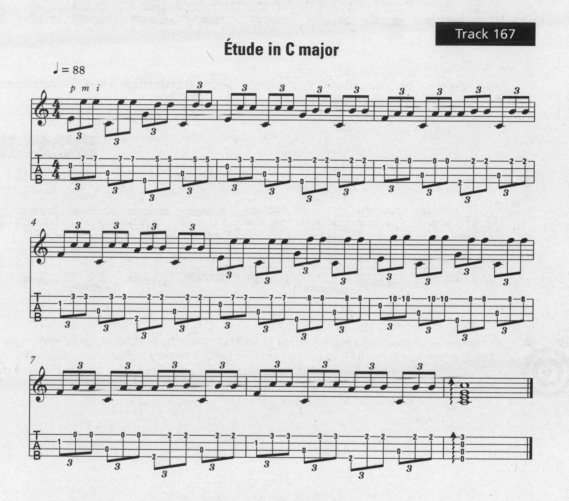

Track 167

Étude in C major

Figuring out four-finger tremolo

For the four-finger tremolo, alternate between plucking the bottom string with your ring, middle and index fingers in that order. Pluck the top three strings with your thumb. First, just assign your thumb to pluck the second string and practise the tremolo on the bottom string.

Track 168

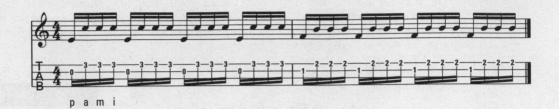

Now, alternate your thumb between plucking the top three strings while maintaining the tremolo on the bottom string.

Track 169

Compose your own intricate-sounding fingerstyle piece by writing out your own chord progression and using the four-finger tremolo technique to play it. For some inspiration, look up Francisco Tárrega's 'Recuerdos de la Alhambra', one of the most popular and beautiful guitar pieces ever written that uses the four-finger tremolo. It's insane.

Chapter 10

Taking a Deeper Look at Single-Note Fingerpicking Techniques

In This Chapter

▶ Learning intricate fingerstyle pieces from Bach and Carulli

▶ Practising alternation and articulation techniques to navigate single-note passages

▶ Strumming and fingerpicking the melody of a song

*I*n the last couple of chapters, I've focused on forms of fingerpicking that feature a repetitive pattern throughout an entire song or piece of music, whether it's a rhythmic fingerpicking pattern (Chapter 8), arpeggio or tremolo (Chapter 9). In this chapter, you look at fingerstyle pieces that require your picking hand to perform intricate single-note passages. A *single-note passage* is a succession of single, individual notes plucked on the same string, oftentimes the melody line of the song. This is different than the fingerpicking patterns taught in Chapters 8 and 9 because the order in which you pluck the notes of a single-note passage with your picking hand varies throughout a piece of music, which means there isn't a continuous, repetitive picking pattern. Because of this, fingerpicking pieces that feature single-note passages demand more dexterity, readiness and fluidity from your picking hand.

The exercises you practise in this chapter help improve your fingerpicking technique so you can easily navigate those more difficult, single-note passages in any piece of music. First, you study four different types of alternation, where you pluck the same string with multiple fingers, which allows you to fingerpick single-note passages faster and easier. Then, you practise exercises that help make your single-note picking more expressive. Lastly, you combine strumming chords and fingerpicking to play solo instrumental versions of songs that would normally be sung.

Learning a solo fingerpicking piece on the ukulele takes a fair amount of time to get it sounding just right. Be patient with yourself as you learn and practise the following exercises and pieces. The more your fingers spend time with these, the easier and more natural you find that fingerpicking of all different sorts becomes on the ukulele.

Speeding up Single-Note Passages

The following exercises help improve playing and fingerpicking single-note passages with your fretting hand and picking hand. These techniques are especially beneficial if you wish to fingerpick instrumental pieces on the ukulele (such as in Chapter 9) or if you wish to solo (such as in Chapter 14).

Practising four alternation techniques

Using *alternation* in your fingerpicking is extremely beneficial for increasing the speed and fluidity of single-note passages in an instrumental piece or solo. Alternation happens when you pluck consecutive notes on the same string with multiple fingers. In the following exercises, I show you four alternation techniques. Of these four, there isn't necessarily one that is better than the other. Through time, experience and practice, you'll find that some of these methods work better in some cases than others.

These exercises are more about working your picking hand rather than worrying about the actual notes you are playing, so these exercises are written in just ukulele tab. In this first exercise, ascend and descend through the first four frets by plucking alternately with your index and middle fingers, in that order. Continue the sequence all the way up the fretboard. This is the most common alternation technique.

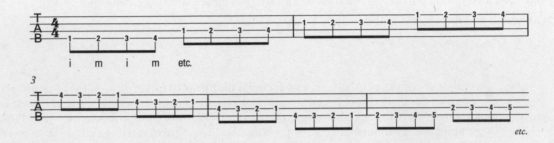

The second alternation technique uses your thumb and index finger. This technique is preferred by many players because the movement tends to be easier, since your thumb and index finger use two different groups of muscles to produce movement.

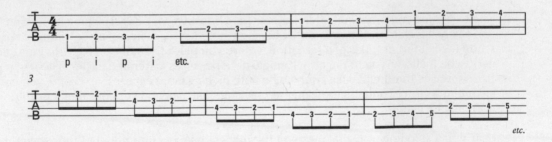

Next, practise using your thumb and middle finger to alternate between the notes. It's always a good idea to practise these sequences in different rhythms, so practise this exercise in a triplet rhythm.

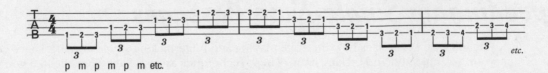

The final alternation technique uses your ring, middle and index fingers. Because this technique doesn't use your thumb, it's especially beneficial in songs where you're playing ascending and descending passages while using your thumb to pluck other notes at the same time. Practise this exercise in a sixteenth note rhythm.

 Continue your practice of these alternation techniques by applying them to any of the scale exercises and sequences in Part IV 'Mastering the Fretboard.'

Applying alternation techniques to pieces of music

The alternation technique you decide to use in an actual piece of music can vary. Through practice, you begin to naturally gravitate towards a certain alternation technique depending on the piece of music and the context of the notes in the song. The following pieces suggest different ways of alternating between single-note passages. Check them out.

Bach's 'Minuet in G'

Chances are you've heard Johann Sebastian Bach's 'Minuet in G' at a wedding or in a film. It's a well-known, famous piece that nearly any listener would recognise, which makes it a great song to add to your repertoire. The piece incorporates simultaneous plucked notes and single-note ascending and descending melody lines that are played on the same string and across multiple strings. Because the notes in the piece are played across all four strings of the ukulele, use the four-finger picking technique where you assign a finger to each string, as described in Chapter 7.

For most of the single-note passages, alternate between plucking the notes with your index (represented by an *i*) and middle (represented by an *m*) fingers, as indicated in the music. For some passages, you might decide to incorporate your ring finger (represented by an *a*) to alternate, but this is up to your experimentation and trial and error. Often times, there isn't a right or wrong way to navigate between single-note passages, like in this piece. The right way is the way that allows you to pluck each note with rhythm and clarity.

 For the first six measures of the song, to avoid jumping around too much, use your fretting hand's index finger to barre the strings on the 5th fret. This means you lay the side of your index finger across the strings to hold down and fret the notes at the 5th fret. If you do this, you're able to maintain this position and reach all of the notes through these measures with your other fingers.

As a clarifying point, Bach composed 'Minuet in G' in the key of G major for the harpsichord. To make the piece accessible for the ukulele, the following arrangement of 'Minuet in G' is written in F major – a more 'ukulele-friendly' key.

Track 170

Minuet in G

Carulli's 'Variations On a Theme, Op. 194'

Fernando Carulli (1770–1841) was one of the greatest Italian composers of his time. He's famous for writing hundreds of classical guitar pieces. 'Variations On a Theme' is sometimes referred to as 'Old French Shepherd's Song'. This beautiful piece features quick single-note passages that separate simultaneously plucked chords to create a melodic but harmonically rich sound.

This piece can be played entirely on the bottom three strings of the ukulele. Keep it simple by assigning your thumb (represented by a *p*) to pluck the third string, index finger (represented by an *i*) to pluck the second string, and middle finger (represented by an *m*) to pluck the first string. First, take a look at the piece of music on the next page, but as you do so, refer to the couple following tips.

The first few measures feature different two-note chords that jump up and down the fretboard. Take a look at the suggested fingerings to discover these moveable positions. These first measures are a musical idea that repeats throughout the entire piece, so once you have it down, you're able to play most of the song.

Next, take a look at measures 11 and 12. These measures require a bit of finesse to navigate smoothly. Pay close attention to the suggested fingering for your fretting hand and alternation in your picking hand. As you practise this section, take it a couple of notes at a time. Give your fingers time to get used to these positions. The more you practise this section the more natural it will come when it comes time to play through the entire song.

The alternation in this piece mostly happens between the middle and index fingers in that order. This is because most of the sequences are descending and start on the bottom string. Because your middle finger is already assigned to pluck the bottom string, it's intuitive to start the alternating single-note sequence with your middle finger. At the same time, don't be afraid to experiment with other ways of alternating your fingers between these notes.

Variations On a Theme, Op. 194

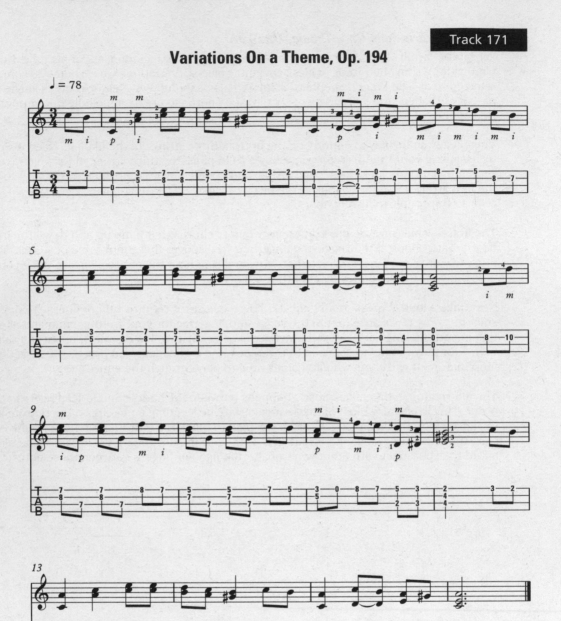

Articulating Single-Note Passages

Articulation refers to the expression you put into executing single-note melody lines and solos. The following exercises address four articulation techniques: hammer-ons, pull-offs, slides and bends. These techniques are commonly used in soloing (like in Chapter 14) and navigating single-note melody lines that show up in instrumental pieces (like in this chapter). Use these exercises to increase the speed, strength and dexterity of your fretting hand.

Hammer-on exercises

Use a *hammer-on* to move up from a lower to a higher note on a string while only plucking the string once. For example, press down your index finger on the 1st fret of the bottom string. Pluck the bottom string like normal, and while the string is ringing, in one quick motion, press down your middle finger on the 2nd fret of the bottom string. When done correctly, the note on the 2nd fret of the bottom string should ring out just as clearly as the plucked note on the 1st fret.

For the hammer-on, it might help to imagine pressing your finger through the fretboard to get the string to ring out. Don't be afraid to give the string some pressure.

In this first exercise, start at the 2nd fret and practise hammering-on across all four strings. To begin, hammer-on from your index to middle finger, index to ring finger and index to little finger.

Track 172

Next, hammer-on from your middle to ring finger and then from your middle to little finger. Lastly, practise hammering-on from your ring to little finger. This last part is tough, but it's absolutely perfect for building up strength in your little finger.

Track 173

The hammer-on can also be used to transition between multiple notes. In this exercise, first practise hammering-on multiple notes using your index, middle and ring fingers, and then hammer-on multiple notes using your middle, ring and little fingers.

Track 174

Pull-off exercises

A *pull-off* is the opposite of a hammer-on. Use a pull-off to move down from a higher note to a lower note on a string while only plucking the string once. For example, place your middle finger on the 5th fret of the third string. At the same time, place your index finger on the 4th fret of the same string, right behind your middle finger. With both fingers pressed down on the fretboard, pluck the third string to sound the note on the 5th fret, and right after you do so, pull down across the third string with your middle finger to sound the note on the 4th fret.

In this previous example, don't just lift up your middle finger off the string to perform the pull-off. To produce the clearest sound, think about pulling down across the string with your middle finger as if you were plucking the string.

For this first exercise, practise performing a variety of different pull-offs. Start off pulling-off from your middle to index finger; then, pull-off from your ring to index finger; and lastly, pull-off from your little finger to index finger.

Track 175

In the following exercise, practise pulling-off from your ring to middle finger, and then, your little to middle finger. Lastly, practise pulling-off from your little to ring finger.

Track 176

Practise the pull-off technique across multiple notes. The following exercise first practises pull-offs using your ring, middle and index fingers, and then, using your little, ring and middle fingers.

Track 177

Slide exercises

A *slide* works in one of two ways: up or down. To slide up, place your middle finger on the 3rd fret of the bottom string. With your finger held down, pluck the bottom string, and right after you do so, slide up your middle finger up to the 4th fret, while still pressing down on the string. To slide down, with your middle finger on the 4th fret of the bottom string, pluck the string and slide your finger down to the 3rd fret, while keeping pressure on the string with your finger. Slides not only add character to a single-note passage, but they also string together multiple notes in a seamless way.

In this first exercise, practise sliding up a half step from the 5th to 6th fret on each string, and then, down a half step from the 6th to 5th fret on each string. Make it your goal to play this exercise with each finger: index, middle, ring and little.

Track 178

For this exercise, practise sliding up and down a whole step. Again, practise this exercise with all four fingers.

Track 179

The goal is to make the note you are sliding to ring out nearly as loud as the initial plucked note. There shouldn't be a drastic difference between the two notes. To do this, ensure that you are maintaining constant pressure on the string throughout the entire slide. Don't be afraid to press down a little harder than you normally would to fret a chord.

Bend exercises

To perform a *bend*, push a string across the fretboard to increase the pitch by adding tension to the string. The trick is to use multiple fingers to push the string across the fretboard. For example, to bend the second string on the 6th fret up a *half step* (one fret higher), first, place your ring finger on the 6th fret of the second string, with your index and middle fingers placed right behind on the same string. With all of these fingers pressed against the string, push the string up across the fretboard until the pitch matches that of the note on the 7th fret of the second string. To bend the note up a *whole step* (two frets higher), bend the string farther until it matches the pitch of the note on the 8th fret of the second string.

For bends on the bottom two strings (the A-string and E-string), push the string up across the fretboard. For bends on the top two strings (the g-string and C-string), push the string down across the fretboard.

In this first exercise, practise bending notes up a half step on the 7th fret of each string. This means you bend the note until it matches the pitch of the note on the 8th fret of the string, as if it were plucked normally.

Track 180

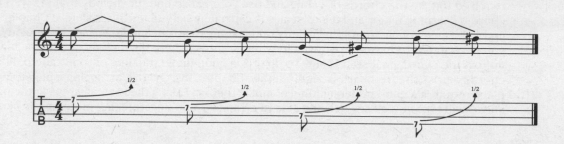

Now, practise bending the notes up a whole step on the 7th fret of each string. This means the bent note should match the pitch of the note on the 9th fret of the string.

Track 181

Because of the amount of force a bend requires on the strings of the ukulele, it's not uncommon on even a higher quality ukulele for the string to go out of tune after you bend it. If this happens to you, don't be afraid to substitute a slide for a bend.

Strumming and Fingerpicking for Melody

If you don't consider yourself the best singer, one of the best ways to find your 'voice' through the ukulele is to pluck the melody of a song while strumming. Taking songs that are normally sung and strummed and turning them into an intricate fingerpicking arrangement puts an exciting new twist on a song.

You might be wondering how you can take a song that is normally sung and make it into a solo fingerpicking arrangement. The easiest way is to search the internet for ukulele tabs.

Chances are someone has already tabbed out an arrangement of the song you're interested in playing. The online ukulele community is one of the nicest and most generous communities you'll ever meet. There are some extremely talented ukulele players who've taken the time to arrange different solo fingerpicking pieces for the ukulele. My favourites are: Al Wood from Ukulele Hunt (`ukulelehunt.com`), Dominator's Ukulele Tabs (`dominator.ukeland.com`), and Roger Ruthen from PDF Minstrel (`pdfminstrel.wordpress.com`).

The second way is to come up with your own fingerpicking arrangements. To do this, you're required to take the chords of a song and use your ear to find the melody that fits with those chords. Learning major and minor scales is especially helpful for this task (see Chapters 11 and 12). Once you've found the melody of the song, to strum and fingerpick the melody, you're required to harmonise the melody into chords, where the melody note is the highest note in the chord, so it stands out. To do this, a good understanding of triads and building chords across the fretboard is required (see Chapter 13). Overall, arranging a fingerpicking piece requires a good understanding of music theory. Taking these small steps in the pages ahead will take you closer to being able to arrange a solo fingerpicking piece on the ukulele.

Playing 'Silent Night'

To strum and fingerpick the melody of a song at the same time (the notes that are normally sung), add strums to certain notes of the song to create fullness and richness to the sound. To make the melody of the song stand out, for strummed chords, place the melody note as the highest note in the chord. This means some of the chords in 'Silent Night' might look a little different than what you are used to. Use the fingering numbers to discover how to fret these chords.

In the following arrangement, strums happen on the first beat of the measure since this is the strongest beat of the measure. The squiggly arrow in the ukulele tab indicates which way to strum across the strings. An arrow pointing up, like in measure 5, indicates a down strum, while an arrow pointing down, like in measure 1, indicates an up strum.

The reason you would choose an up strum over a down strum is so you can ensure that the melody note is the last note ringing out in the strummed chord, to make it stand out to your listener. For example, in measure 1, it works best to perform an up strum instead of a down strum, because this allows the highest note in the chord to ring out last (in this case, the fourth string – the g-string). In measure 5, it works best to perform a down strum, because this allows the highest note in the chord to ring out last (in this case, the 5th fret of the first string – the A-string).

For down strums, use the flesh side of your thumb, and for up strums, use the flesh side of your index finger. You might decide to pluck the individual notes with your thumb or index finger. I prefer to use my thumb to pluck individual notes because it gives the fullest tone (to my ears). However, in songs with faster fingerpicking patterns, you might incorporate some of the alternation techniques you practised earlier in this chapter.

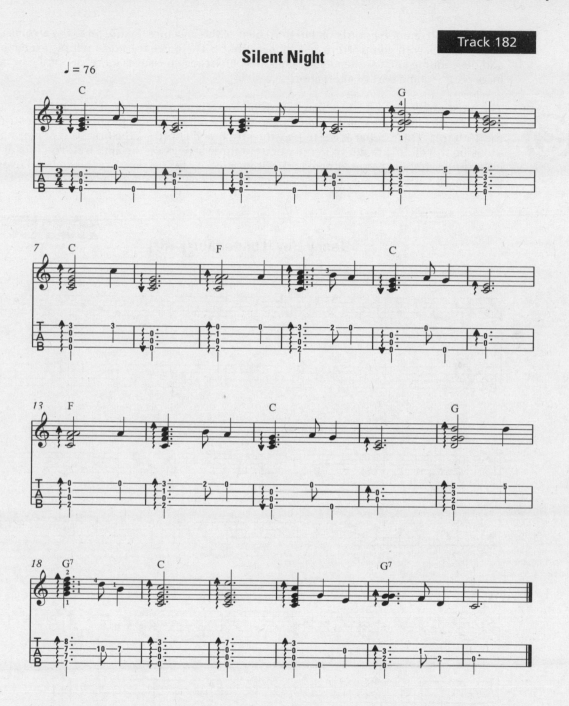

Silent Night

Track 182

Playing 'Danny Boy (Londonderry Air)'

Continue to practise strumming and fingerpicking the melody of a song by learning the classic, Irish tune 'Danny Boy', also known as 'Londonderry Air'. The arrangement features strummed chords throughout the song on the first beats of the measure, with some additional strummed chords on the third beat of the measure. Nearly all of the strums are down strums with an up strum only in measure 24. The piece features multiple ascending and descending single-note melody lines. To pluck these passages more smoothly, be sure to incorporate some sort of alternation.

The most challenging part to 'Danny Boy' happens in measure 26 and 27. For the last note in measure 26, I like to use my middle finger to barre or hold down the bottom three strings at the 10th fret. This prepares me to play the strummed chord on the first beat of measure 27. By using the middle finger to fret the bottom three strings on the 10th fret, you free up your index finger to play the next note at the 8th fret of the first string. Try this out and even experiment with your own finger positions to see what works best for you.

Track 183

Danny Boy (Londonderry Air)

Part IV
Mastering the Ukulele Fretboard

*Five Great Ways to Develop
Your Fretboard Skills*

- **Build major and minor triads.** A *triad* is just a fancy name for a chord made up of three notes. Each type of triad has its own distinct sound and mood, just like scales. Learn how to build a range of different triads.

- **Combine different kinds of triad.** Kick it up a notch and practise switching between major and minor triads in different ways across the fretboard. Use actual songs to work out how.

- **Turn triads into moveable chords.** Move on up from three-string triads to the mysteries of the moveable chord, where you use all four fingers to create the sound.

- **Get jazzy with moveable seventh chords.** Seventh chords are built around major and minor triads, but they have an added note that gives them a jazzier sound. Get to grips with seventh chords of different types and then practise playing a couple popular jazz chord progressions.

- **Progress with chord progressions.** Write out your own chord progressions in your practice journal and practise cycling through the different triad inversions for each chord.

Go to www.dummies.com/go/ukuleleexercises to listen to audio tracks.

In this part . . .

- ✔ Build major and minor scales across the neck of the ukulele.

- ✔ Come to grips with intervals, triads and chords.

- ✔ Understand how notes relate to each other by building chords.

- ✔ Pick up new soloing techniques.

- ✔ Learn how to diversify your ukulele sound.

- ✔ Go to www.dummies.com/go/ukuleleexercises to hear the classic 'When the Saints Go Marching In' (Track 203; described in Chapter 11) played on the uke.

Chapter 11

Learning the Fretboard with Major Scales

· ·

· ·

*O*ne of the best things about the ukulele is that it's not a very intimidating instrument. You can pick it up, and with a few simple chords, you're able to play all sorts of songs. So, why in the world would you want to learn the ukulele fretboard? What's the big deal?

First and foremost, learning the ukulele fretboard allows you to gain an understanding of the music that you are making. This understanding is powerful because it equips you to create music in new and different ways, and unlock parts of playing the ukulele that might not have seemed possible. For example, if you're familiar with the fretboard, you're able to come up with alternate chord positions to add variety to a song. If you don't have a lot of confidence as a singer, you can use your knowledge of the fretboard to arrange an intricate fingerpicking piece that highlights the melody of a song, which would normally be sung. Maybe you're just tired of looking at a piece of music and fumbling your way around trying to find the right notes. By understanding the ukulele through the fretboard, you're able to experience the instrument in a whole new way.

There are two popular ways to approach learning the fretboard. The first way involves going up and down every string and memorising every single note on every single fret. If you're superhuman and have a photographic memory, this is the way for you! If you're like me, I didn't find learning the fretboard like this to be very beneficial.

The second way to the learn the notes of the fretboard involves studying the relationships between notes and the sounds they make – not just brute force memorisation. One of the best ways to do this is through the study and practical application of scales. A *scale* is a collection of notes arranged in ascending or descending order by pitch. Entire songs are based around various scales. As you study different scales and the notes that make up each one, you begin to have a more comprehensive and holistic understanding of what is actually going on underneath your fingertips, rather than it just being a bunch of random notes.

In this chapter, you start making sense and navigating across the ukulele fretboard through the study of major scales. Most songs are built around the major scale, which makes it one of the most fundamental scales to get under your fingertips. The first few exercises in this chapter exercise your brain and then you move on to practising the ideas you've picked up through scale patterns and sequences. My goal isn't just to teach you a bunch of patterns across the fretboard. At the end of the chapter, you take your understanding of the fretboard and play two actual pieces of music using the major scale.

Taking a Quick Look at the Chromatic Scale

In order to build a scale, you have to know what notes are available to use. It's like painting a picture – in order to paint something beautiful, you have to have the right colours. To do that, first meet the *chromatic scale*.

You can only play twelve notes on the ukulele – no more, no less. So when building a scale, you have to select from these twelve notes. Arrange all of these notes in ascending and descending order by pitch and you have the chromatic scale.

You can play a chromatic scale by starting on any string and moving up one fret at a time all the way up the neck. Since a chromatic scale contains every possible note you could play on the ukulele, it doesn't matter what note you start on. For now, just play a chromatic scale on the C-string of the ukulele, as shown in this figure.

This figure shows every and any note you could ever play on the ukulele. These same notes repeat themselves in different places and at different octaves on the other strings.

As you can see, notes are represented by the first seven letters of the alphabet: A, B, C, D, E, F, G. These letters by themselves, without any symbols next to them, are called *natural* notes.

Sharps (#) and flats (♭) modify natural notes by raising or lowering the note a half step (one fret). For example, if you add a sharp to a C note, the pitch is raised a half step and becomes a C#. If you add a flat to a D note, the pitch is lowered a half step and becomes a D♭. As you can see in the examples for the previous figure, in terms of pitch, a C# and D♭ are the same note. The notes with sharps and flats, like 'C#/D♭,' are *enharmonic* notes. This means C# and D♭ are separate notes but they are identical in terms of pitch. How they're referred to depends on the key of a song.

The most important notes to focus on are the seven natural notes (the ones without sharps and flats). Don't get lost in all the sharps and flats. If you can find the natural notes on the fretboard, it's easy to fill in the blanks with the enharmonic notes. To start finding the seven natural notes on the fretboard, build a major scale, the most important scale of all.

Building a Major Scale

A *major scale* is made up of seven different notes. The vast majority of songs are built around the major scale, which makes it one of the most essential scales to know. It's easy to create a major scale in any of the twelve keys with a simple pattern.

Learning the major scale interval pattern

An *interval* refers to the space or distance between two different notes. There are many different types of intervals. The two intervals that are important to know are half step and whole step intervals, as demonstrated in the next figure.

A half step interval is just one fret away from whatever note you are on. A whole step interval is two frets away from whatever note you are on.

The major scale is based around a half step, whole step interval pattern: **whole**, **whole**, **half**, **whole**, **whole**, **whole**, **half**. This means you can start on any of the twelve notes in a chromatic scale and apply this pattern to build a major scale.

I'm going to show you how to use this interval pattern to build a C major scale – the king of all major scales. Return to the chromatic scale, start on a C note (the *root note* of a C major scale), and apply this half step, whole step interval pattern, as shown in the next figure. Circled letters indicate notes that fall within this major scale pattern.

To break this down even further, a **whole step** up from the starting C note is D. A **whole step** up from D is E. A **half step** up from E is F. A **whole step** up from F is G. A **whole step** up from

G is A. A **whole step** up from A is B, and lastly, a **half step** up from B returns you to the root note of the scale, C.

As you can see, a C major scale uses all natural notes (no sharps and flats), which makes it the best scale to learn as you learn the fretboard. To play a C major scale on the ukulele, start on the open C-string of your ukulele and use the half step, whole step interval pattern, as demonstrated in the next figure.

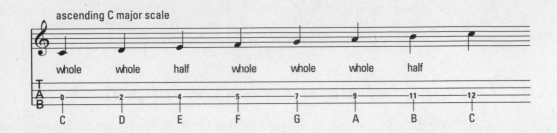

For now, just practise the C major scale on the C-string. In a short bit, you learn how to play a C major scale across the different strings of the ukulele.

Creating a major scale in any key

Using the major scale's half step, whole step interval pattern, you are able to build a major scale in any key. The next scale you build is a G major scale. As before, take the chromatic scale, but this time, start on a G note (or in this case, the top g-string), and apply the half step, whole step major scale interval pattern, as shown here.

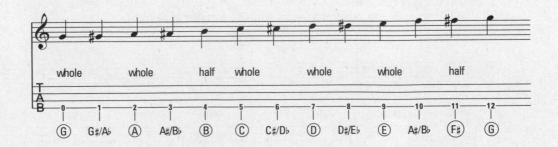

A **whole step** up from the starting G note is A. A **whole step** up from A is B. A **half step** up from B is C. A **whole step** up from C is D. A **whole step** up from D is E. A **whole step** up from E is F#, and lastly, a **half step** up from F# returns you to the root note of the scale, G.

In the next exercise, play a G major scale on the top g-string of the ukulele.

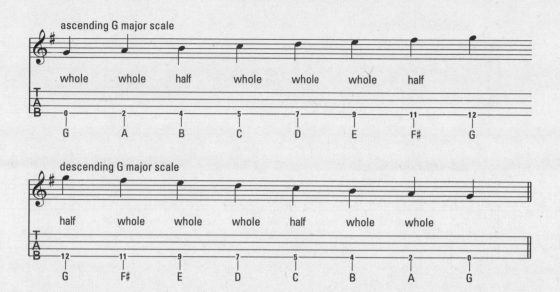

ascending G major scale

whole   whole   half   whole   whole   whole   half

G   A   B   C   D   E   F#   G

descending G major scale

half   whole   whole   whole   half   whole   whole

G   F#   E   D   C   B   A   G

You might be wondering why you don't refer to the F# note in the G major scale as 'Gb.' After all, they are the same note, right? This is true, but if you were to refer to F# as 'Gb' you would end up with two 'G' notes – G and Gb – and consequently, there would be no 'F' note. For clarity's sake, it's best to have all note letters present in a major scale and not to double up on any of the letters. In this way, it's better to use F#.

Next, build an F major scale by starting on the F note in a chromatic scale (the 1st fret of the E-string), as shown here.

whole   whole   half   whole   whole   whole   half

F   F#/Gb   G   G#/Ab   A   Bb   B   C   C#/Db   D   D#/Eb   E   F

A **whole step** up from the starting F note is G. A **whole step** up from G is A. A **half step** up from A is Bb. A **whole step** up from Bb is C. A **whole step** up from C is D. A **whole step** up from D is E, and lastly, a **half step** up from E returns you to the root note of the scale, F.

Build an F major scale on your ukulele by starting on the F note on the 1st fret of the second string, as demonstrated here.

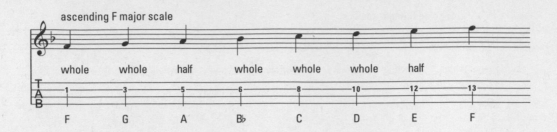

ascending F major scale

whole   whole   half   whole   whole   whole   half

F   G   A   B♭   C   D   E   F

descending F major scale

half   whole   whole   whole   half   whole   whole

F   E   D   C   B♭   A   G   F

Practising Major Scale Patterns in Three Different Keys

It's time to put your understanding of major scales into action! As you've probably found, it's not very practical to build and play a major scale on only one string. It's faster and more efficient to learn a major scale in different positions. This allows you to keep your fingers in the same area while still hitting all the notes in the scale across multiple strings.

For each major scale pattern, there is a neck diagram, music and tab notation. Follow the suggested fingering for the scale pattern and notice where the root note of the scale falls within the pattern (represented by a black dot). If you can identify the root note in the scale pattern, you can slide the entire pattern up and down across the fretboard to play in other keys, as I will show you in a little bit.

Don't just learn the patterns. Engage your mind in the process of learning and remembering the notes in each scale too. Practise saying them out loud as you pluck each note. Patterns are extremely beneficial but knowing what you're playing is even more beneficial in the long run.

Learning natural notes with C major

Practising the C major scale is one of the most beneficial exercises for learning the ukulele fretboard. Since the scale only uses natural notes (no sharps and flats), it gives you a great foundation for building all different types of scales.

Position #1: C major scale

The first position takes advantage of the open strings of the ukulele. Since the strings of the ukulele are tuned to notes that are found in the key of C major, you can use these open strings as a part of your C major scale pattern.

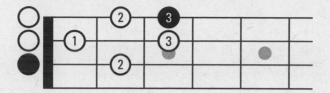

Track 184

Position #2: C major scale

Notice that this position starts on a D note rather than a C note. Even though you're starting on a note other than the root note of the scale, the position is still a C major scale because all of the notes in a C major scale are being played.

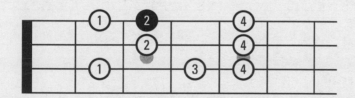

Track 185

Position #3: C major scale

This position is a little trickier than the previous ones, so take it slowly at first. To play the notes on the bottom two strings, shift your fingers to hover over the 5th to 8th frets. On the ascending pattern, as soon as your little finger plays the 7th fret of the third string, start moving your index finger up a fret to get ready to play the 5th fret of the second string. On the descending pattern, as soon as your index finger plays the 5th fret of the second string, slide your little finger down a fret to get it in position to play the 7th fret of the third string.

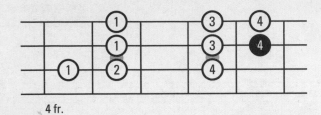

4 fr.

Track 186

E F G A B Ⓒ D E F E D Ⓒ B A G F E

Position #4: C major scale

When you get this high up the neck of the ukulele, things start to get a little bit cramped because the frets get narrower. Most of the time, you'll probably make the most use out of the notes in the 1st, 2nd and 3rd positions, but the notes this high up the neck can be advantageous to use for something like a solo since they are higher in pitch and tend to stand out more.

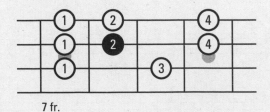

7 fr.

Track 187

G A B Ⓒ D E F G F E D Ⓒ B A G

C major scale in all positions

The next figure shows the C major scale in all positions across the ukulele fretboard, including the top g-string. When practising scales, it's a bit awkward to incorporate the top g-string into the patterns, since it breaks the ascending and descending sound of the scale. However, after you get a good sense of all the scale positions, it's easy enough to incorporate the notes from the top g-string that fit within the C major scale.

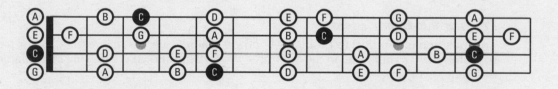

Seeing how sharps work with G major

Once you know the C major scale patterns, it's easy to modify them to change them into major scales in other keys. Next, take a C major scale and turn it into a G major scale. There are two ways of doing this:

- ✔ Identify the 'C' root note in the C major scale patterns (represented by a black dot) and slide the entire pattern shape to a different place on the fretboard, so the root note of the pattern is pressing down on a 'G' note.

- ✔ Since you built a G major scale earlier in this chapter, you know there is an F# note in the key of G major. To turn the C major scale patterns into G major, raise all the F notes up a half step to make them F#.

It's best to use a combination of these ideas. You'll find that some of the G major pattern shapes are the same patterns you used to play in C major, however, it's good to be aware of the notes you are playing on the fretboard too.

Position #1: G major scale

All of the open strings on the ukulele are notes that are found in a G major scale, so you can make use of them in this first position. Notice that this position is nearly identical to position #1 of the C major scale. The only difference is that in the G major scale, the F note is raised a half step (up one fret) to play an F#. This small, simple change turns the pattern from being in C major to G major.

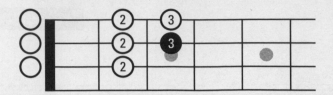

Track 188

C D E F# Ⓖ A B C B A Ⓖ F# E D C

Position #2: G major scale

This position is identical to position #4 of the C major scale. Just move the C major pattern to match the 'G' root note on the 3rd fret of the E-string and you're playing in a completely different key. Easy-peasy!

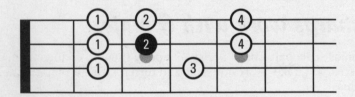

Track 189

D E F# Ⓖ A B C D C B A Ⓖ F# E D

Position #3: G major scale

This position makes a slight shift mid-ways through, which presents a small challenge. In the ascending pattern, as soon as your little finger plays the 7th fret of the third string, shift your index finger up to get ready to play the 5th fret of the second string. On the descending pattern, as soon as your index finger plays the 5th fret on the second string, move your little finger down to get ready to play the 7th fret of the third string.

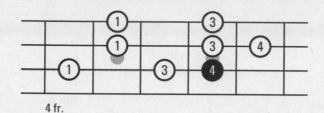

Track 190

Position #4: G major scale

This is another pattern that was used in the C major scale (position #1), but when the position is moved to line up with a different root note, it sounds in G major.

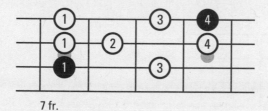

7 fr.

Track 191

G major scale in all positions

The next figure shows the G major scale in all positions across the ukulele fretboard.

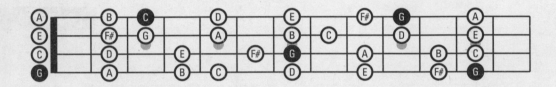

Figuring out flats with F major

Earlier in this chapter, you built an F major scale and discovered that there is a B♭ note in the scale. Simply take the C major scale patterns and lower all the B notes a half step (down one fret) to make them B♭. Voila! You're playing the F major scale up and down the neck of the ukulele.

Position #1: F major scale

Compare this position with position #1 of a C major scale. It's very similar. For this pattern, the B note is lowered a half step to B♭ to make the pattern in F major.

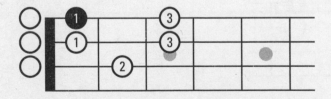

Track 192

Position #2: F major scale

This is another one of those weird jumps that happen between the third and second strings. For the ascending pattern, as you play the 5th fret of the third string, get your index finger ready by shifting it up a fret to play the 3rd fret of the second string. On the descending pattern, as you play the 3rd fret of the second string, get your little finger ready to shift down and play the 5th fret of the third string.

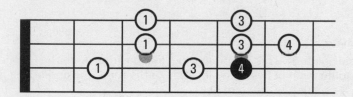

Track 193

Position #3: F major scale

Are you noticing some repeating scale patterns yet? This pattern is just like position #4 of the G major scale, just moved down two frets.

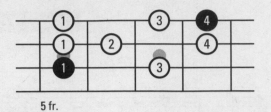

5 fr.

Ⓕ G A B♭ C D E Ⓕ E D C B♭ A G Ⓕ

Position #4: F major scale

Yet another repeated scale pattern. This position is just like position #2 of the C major scale and position. Notice the difference between the location of the root note and how it is shifted to form a major scale in a completely different key.

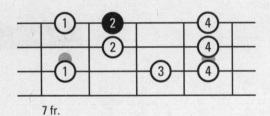

7 fr.

G A B♭ C D E Ⓕ G Ⓕ E D C B♭ A G

F major scale in all positions

This figure shows the F major scale in all positions across the ukulele fretboard.

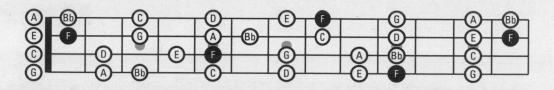

Getting Your Fingers Moving with Major Scale Sequences

When it comes to performing or soloing over actual songs, it's rare that you're constantly ascending and descending a scale pattern. Part of sounding musically interesting is skipping around to different notes. Sequences challenge your fingers to make those not-so-common movements that often come up when playing an actual song.

 To get the most out of the following sequences, pick just a couple to focus on at a time. As you play through each sequence, think about making each note sound as clean as possible. Start slow and work on making the sequence steady and consistent in timing and in volume. Don't forget to practise these at soft and loud volumes too.

The first sequence pattern is in position #1 of the C major scale. Ascend and descend throughout the scale in groups of four notes. Pay attention to the fingering numbers next to the note to get an idea of which finger to use to fret the string.

Track 196

 To switch between notes in this sequence faster and smoother, pluck the notes alternating between your index and middle finger. For example, pluck the first note in the sequence with your index finger, the second note with your middle finger, the third note with your index finger – and so on. For more on alternation techniques, check out Chapter 10.

Here's another sequence in position #1 of the C major scale. This sequence keeps you on your toes a little bit more because the notes switch back and forth more frequently.

Track 197

The next sequence is like the first one, but you start to make use of your little finger using position #2 of the G major scale. Notice too that in the second to last measure of the descending pattern there is a finger jump between the third and second strings. Your index finger is required to jump the strings from the 2nd fret of the third string to the 2nd fret of the second string. To make this change smoother, you might use your index finger to barre, or hold down together, both the third and second strings on the 2nd fret.

Track 198

Play the following sequence in position #3 of the F major scale. Thankfully, there are no skips or jumps across strings, but this pattern does make good use of all four fingers.

Track 199

Stay in position #3 of the F major scale, however, in this sequence, practise some more finger jumps. Right at the start, in the first measure, there is a finger jump. Once you get past that, it's not so bad. There is only one more jump in the second to last measure of the descending pattern. Again, it's okay if you use your index finger to barre these strings.

Track 200

This last sequence combines multiple positions in the G major scale. The sequence starts in position #2. However, in the final measures, you navigate up to higher G major scale positions on the fretboard. Take this pattern slow at first and notice the suggested fingerings for the final measures. In songs, more often than not, you have to break the scale position's suggested fingering to navigate between more difficult passages.

Track 201

Faking Fretboard Knowledge

In addition to your growing knowledge of major scales, the following shortcuts help make locating the right notes across the ukulele fretboard even faster and easier.

Recognising fretboard landmarks

Across the fretboard, there are a few key spots or 'landmarks' for groups of notes. The first is located at the 5th fret. On most ukuleles, there is a dot or a marker on in the middle of the 5th fret. Make it your goal to memorise the notes at the 5th fret across all four strings, as shown in the following figure.

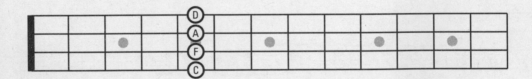

To help remember the notes C-F-A-D, come up with a bizarre acronym like: **C**razy **F**riends **A**re **D**elightful (the weirder the acronym the better – it's easier to remember!). Since the notes C-F-A-D are natural notes (no sharps or flats), if you can find these notes, it can make identifying other nearby notes easier.

The second landmark is at the 7th fret. As you did for the 5th fret, come up with an acronym for the notes on the 7th fret, as shown in the following figure. I like to go more inspirational and motivational with this one: **D**o **G**ood, **B**e **E**xtraordinary.

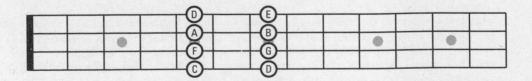

The last landmark is at the 12th fret. By now, you should know that each string of the ukulele is tuned from the top to bottom string: g-C-E-A (see Chapter 1 for information about tuning the ukulele). At the 12th fret, these notes repeat themselves at an octave higher, as shown in the following figure.

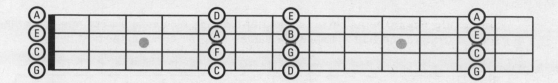

Locating the same note on different strings

There are notes across the ukulele fretboard that can be played on multiple different strings. If you know where one note is, it's easy to find the same note on a different string by using the following tricks. Take a look at the following figure to see how to find the same note on the top and bottom strings.

Each of these figures shows a pattern that can be moved up and down the fretboard to locate other notes. For example, if you move the previous position in the previous figure down two frets to the 3rd fret of the bottom string and the 5th fret of the top string, you are playing the same C note across both strings.

In the next figure, find the same note across the third and fourth strings. If you start on a C note on the 5th fret of the top string, go up seven frets, and pluck the third string at the 12th fret, you are playing the same C note.

If you start on the B note on the 7th fret of the second string, go down five frets, and pluck the bottom string at the 2nd fret, you are playing the same B note, as shown in the following figure.

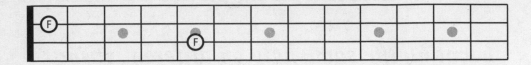

Start on the F note on the 5th fret of the third string, go down four frets, and pluck the second string at the 1st fret to play the same F note, as shown in the next figure.

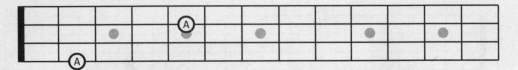

For this pattern, start on the A note on the 2nd fret of the top string, move up three frets, and pluck the second string at the 5th fret to play the same A note, as shown in the following figure.

Line up these patterns with other notes to find the same note across two different strings.

Finding octave notes

The following figures show how to find the same note an octave higher or lower on a different string. Again, these positions can be moved up and down the fretboard to find other octave notes.

Check out the following figure to find the octave of a note that falls on the first or third strings. Start on the F note on the 5th fret of the third string, move up three frets, and pluck the bottom string at the 8th fret to play the same F note an octave higher.

While a bit more spread out, find the octave of a note on the bottom two strings, as shown in the next figure. Start on the A note on the 5th fret of the second string, move up seven frets, and pluck the bottom string at the 12th fret to play the same A note.

Using Major Scales to Play Actual Songs

Most music that has been written has been based around the major scale. With just a few scale positions and some scale sequences under your belt, you have the ability to play the melody of thousands of different songs. Put your major scales to work to play a couple songs right now.

Playing 'Angels We Have Heard On High'

'Angels We Have Heard On High' is a lively Christmas carol featuring a high soaring, repeating, eighth note descending melody line about half way through the song. It's an extremely fun song to play because there is a fair amount of movement in the melody. As you can see, there are multiple phrases in this song that repeat. So once you've learned a part of the song, you've almost learned the entire piece.

To play this carol, use position #3 of the F major scale, starting with your index finger. This position can be used to play the entire song.

Track 202

Angels We Have Heard On High

Playing 'When the Saints Go Marching In'

The song 'When the Saints Go Marching In' was originally used as a funeral march for the procession of coffins to the cemetery. However, when jazz bands started playing the song around the 1930s and 1940s, more upbeat renditions of this song were popularised. The song's syncopated melody lends itself well to being played at faster tempos.

Take position #3 of the F major scale that you used in 'Angels We Have Heard On High', slide it down three frets, and play this song in the key of D major. The most challenging aspect to this song is that there are a lot of finger jumps, where you are taking the same finger and playing two adjacent strings on the same fret. To make these jumps smoother, take your index finger and barre a portion of the 2nd fret. Take it slow at first and then speed it up into your own upbeat, snappy version!

Track 203

When the Saints Go Marching In

Chapter 12

Taking On Three Minor Scales

● ●

In This Chapter

▶ Playing natural, harmonic or melodic minor scales

▶ Discovering how minor and major scales are related

▶ Applying minor scales to play actual songs

● ●

*T*he minor scale is the major scale's darker counterpart. Where a major scale is considered happy, joyful and upbeat, a minor scale is often felt as being sad, dark and even brooding. Songs written in minor keys are some of the most beautiful ever written. The darker sound of a minor scale has the ability to communicate complex feelings that you can't always communicate through a major key.

Three different types of minor scales exist: *natural*, *harmonic* and *melodic*. All three are worth learning because each has a distinctive sound and mood, so much so that entire songs have been written around each one. Feel free to skip ahead and take a listen to the songs at the end of this chapter to hear the sound of the different minor scales.

In this chapter, you learn how to build the three different types of minor scales in any key. In addition, you practise playing minor scales in various positions across the ukulele fretboard. Lastly, you discover how to differentiate between the sound of each of the three different types of minor scales by playing three well-known songs.

Learning scales falls into two parts: the pattern of the scale and the actual notes of the scale. Like major scales, minor scale positions show repeated patterns throughout different keys across the fretboard. Pay close attention to the root note in each of these patterns; you can shift the pattern to play in a different minor key by lining the root note up with a different note. At the same time, don't just learn the patterns. Be sure to engage your mind and think about the notes you're plucking in each pattern. While patterns are essential, understanding the relationships between the notes makes you a stronger ukulele player in the long run.

Don't try to learn all three minor scales at once. Just focus on one at a time and spend as much time as you need to learn the scale before moving on to the next. I recommend starting with the natural minor scale.

Building a Natural Minor Scale

Your quest to conquer all three different types of minor scales (natural, harmonic and melodic) starts with the *natural minor scale*, often referred to as just the *minor scale*. It's one of the most widely used minor scales in music, and it's from the natural scale where you're able to build other types of minor scales.

Discovering the natural minor scale interval pattern

Like a major scale (see Chapter 11), a natural minor scale is built on a basic *interval* pattern of half steps and whole steps. An interval is the space between two different notes. A note played a half step higher is one fret higher on the ukulele. A note played a whole step higher is two frets higher.

The natural minor scale is based around the following half step, whole step interval pattern: **whole**, **half**, **whole**, **whole**, **half**, **whole**, **whole**.

First, build a natural minor scale in the key of A. Let me show you how to do this. Start on an 'A' note in a chromatic scale (see Chapter 11 to learn more about the chromatic scale) and apply the above half step, whole step interval pattern to discover the A natural minor scale, as shown in the next figure. Circled notes represent notes that fall within the A natural minor scale.

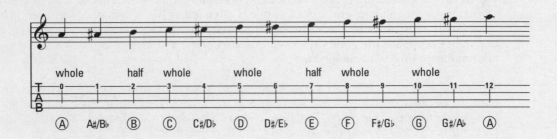

To break this down, a **whole step** up from the starting note A is B. A **half step** up from B is C. A **whole step** up from C is D. A **whole step** up from D is E. A **half step** up from E is F. A **whole step** up from F is G, and lastly, a **whole step** up from G is A, which returns you back to the root note of the scale an octave higher.

To play the A natural minor scale on the ukulele, for now, just play it on the open A-string, as shown in the next figure.

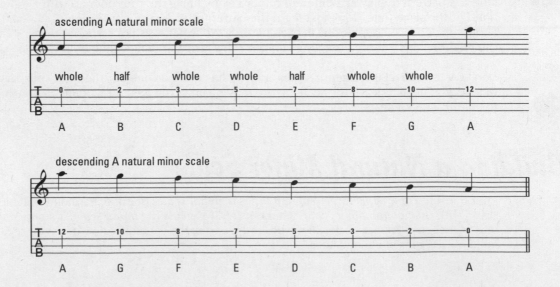

TIP

Build a natural minor scale in any other key by starting on any note in the chromatic scale and applying the natural minor's half step, whole step interval pattern.

Relating natural minor to major

Every scale relates to another scale in some way. If you can see how different types of scales relate to one another, it makes learning them much easier and less overwhelming.

Building a natural minor scale from a major scale

Each major and minor scale contains seven notes. Each of these notes can be assigned a number to represent its respective scale degree. For example, take a C major scale in the next figure. Each note receives a number 1-7 with the 8th note being the octave.

In the natural minor scale, the 3rd, 6th and 7th scale degrees are *flatted* or lowered by a half step. To make a C major scale a C natural minor scale, lower the third, sixth and seventh notes of the scale a half step, as shown in the next figure.

TIP

Therefore, converting a major scale to a natural minor scale requires the following scale degree formula: 1, 2, b3, 4, 5, b6, b7. Take any major scales that you might have built in Chapter 11 and lower the 3rd, 6th and 7th scale degrees a half step (or down one fret) to transform the scale into natural minor.

Harnessing the power of relative minor and major

As you probably noticed, the A natural minor scale earlier in this chapter is made up of all natural notes – notes without any sharps or flats: A, B, C, D, E, F, G. If you recall from Chapter 11, the C major scale uses the exact same notes as A natural minor except the notes are arranged in a different order: C, D, E, F, G, A, B.

This connection between A natural minor and C major is *relative* meaning, C major's *relative minor* is A natural minor, and A natural minor's *relative major* is C major. They are relative because they share the exact same notes.

In this way, natural minor keys are inextricably linked to major keys. For every major key there is a relative minor, and for every minor key, there is a relative major. Table 12-1 shows all twelve major keys and their relative minors.

Table 12-1	Relative Major and Minor Keys
Relative Major Keys	*Relative Natural Minor Keys*
C major	A minor
D♭ major	B♭ minor
D major	B minor
E♭ major	C minor
E major	C# minor
F major	D minor
F#/G♭ major	D#/E♭ minor
G major	E minor
A♭ major	F minor
A major	F# minor
B♭ major	G minor
B major	G# minor

This means that if you know how to play a major scale across the ukulele fretboard, you know how to play that major scale's relative minor scale across the fretboard. Likewise, if you know how to play a natural minor scale, you know how to play that minor scale's relative major scale. Thinking in this way makes learning natural minor scales less intimidating because you're relating everything to major scales.

This little trick only works with natural minor scales. Not to worry though, because there are more tricks you can use when it comes to learning the harmonic and melodic minor scales. More on those later.

Playing the Natural Minor scale

Once you know how relative minors work, you realise that if you learned the C major, G major and F major scale positions in Chapter 11, you already know how to play the relative minor keys of A minor, E minor and D minor across the fretboard. Relative keys share the same notes, so consequently, their patterns across the fretboard will be the same.

To keep things interesting, learn how to play C natural minor in all positions across the ukulele fretboard. Since a natural minor scale is a major scale with lowered 3rd, 6th and 7th scale degrees, modify the C major scale positions you learned in Chapter 11 to make them C natural minor. This means you take a C major scale and make all of the E notes 'E♭,' the A notes 'A♭,' and the B notes 'B♭.'

Position #1: C natural minor

The first position of the C natural minor scale gives you the truest picture of what the minor scale sounds like because the ascending and descending pattern starts on a C and ends on a C – the strongest note of the scale (that is, the root note).

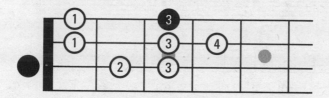

Track 204

Position #2: C natural minor

You know that C natural minor is relative to E♭ major (see Table 12-1). In other words, all of the notes in C minor are used in E♭ major. In this next position, the ascending and descending pattern sounds major because the pattern starts and ends on E♭. While this pattern is representative of E♭ major, it can be seen as another position for C minor because the notes in this position are used in C natural minor. Because this pattern would be used when playing in C minor, notice that the root note 'C' falls on the 3rd fret of the bottom string.

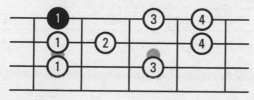

3 fr.

Track 205

Eb F G Ab Bb © D Eb D © Bb Ab G F Eb

Position #3: C natural minor

This position starts and ends on the 4th scale degree of a C natural minor scale - the note 'F'. The root note 'C' falls on the 8th fret of the second string.

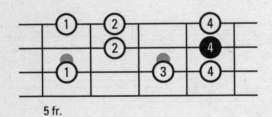

5 fr.

Track 206

F G Ab Bb © D Eb F Eb D © Bb Ab G F

Position #4: C natural minor

TIP

For this next position, in the middle of the pattern you need to reposition your fingers for the notes played on the bottom two strings. In the ascending movement of the scale, after you play the 10th fret on the third string with your little finger, start to move your index finger up to play the 8th fret on the second string. In the descending movement of the scale, after you play the 8th fret on the second string with your index finger, start to move your little finger down to play the 10th fret on the third string.

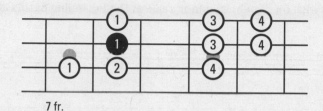

7 fr.

Track 207

G   Ab   Bb   Ⓒ   D   Eb   F   G   Ab   G   F   Eb   D   Ⓒ   Bb   Ab   G

C natural minor in all positions

The next figure shows the C natural minor scale in all positions across the ukulele fretboard.

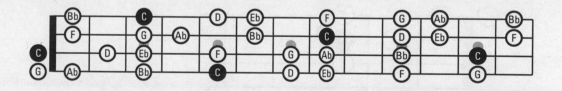

Homing In On Harmonic Minor

Once you have the hang of natural minor, it's easy to build a harmonic minor scale. To build a harmonic minor scale, take a natural minor scale and sharp, or raise, the 7th scale degree. Or, take a major scale and flat the 3rd and 6th scale degrees. Converting a major scale to a harmonic minor scale requires the following scale degree formula: 1, 2, b3, 4, 5, b6, 7.

Check out the next figure to see how a C harmonic minor scale is built using the harmonic minor formula. Compare this with the C natural minor scale at the beginning of this chapter.

This slight alteration to the 7th scale degree creates some complexity in the sound that makes the harmonic scale sound a more complex than the plain ol' natural minor scale. You'd be right in saying it sounds 'exotic.'

Practise building a harmonic scale by taking the G major scale positions you learned in Chapter 11 and flat the 3rd and 6th scale degrees to play a G harmonic minor scale. This means you lower all of the B and E notes down a half step (down one fret) so the B notes become 'B♭' and all of the E notes become 'E♭.'

Position #1: G harmonic minor

Although this position starts and ends on a 'C' note, this is still a G harmonic minor position because the notes used in the pattern are all found in a G harmonic minor scale. Note that the root note 'G' finds itself on the 3rd fret of the second string.

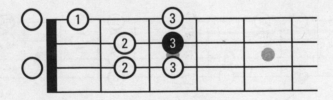

Track 208

C D E♭ F# (G) A B♭ C B♭ A (G) F# E♭ D C

Position #2: G harmonic minor

In a harmonic minor scale there is an interval of one and half steps separating the 6th and 7th scale degrees. So in G harmonic minor, the 'F#' (7th scale degree) is three frets away from the 'E♭' (6th scale degree). This is highlighted in the first two notes of the following scale position.

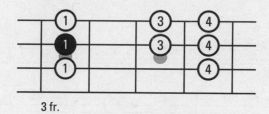

3 fr.

Track 209

E♭ F# (G) A B♭ C D E♭ D C B♭ A (G) F# E♭

Position #3: G harmonic minor

This position gives the truest sound of the harmonic minor scale because the pattern starts and ends on a 'G' note – the strongest note in G harmonic minor (that is, the root note). You'll notice that the three notes that fall on the second string of this pattern require a bit of a stretch. Follow the suggested fingerings and experiment with using your middle or ring finger to fret the 'C' note that falls on the 8th fret of the second string.

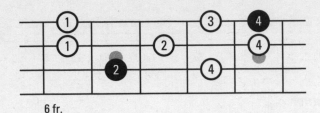

6 fr.

Track 210

 Experiment with moving this position to change to a different key. For example, if you move this exact position down three frets you would be playing in E harmonic minor. This is because you would have lined up the root notes of the pattern to the E notes on the 4th fret of the third string and the 7th fret of the first string.

G harmonic minor in all positions

The next figure shows the G harmonic minor scale in all positions across the ukulele fretboard.

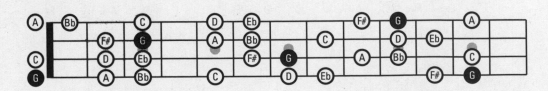

Mixing It Up With Melodic Minor

The melodic minor scale's ascending pattern is different than the descending pattern. The ascending pattern of the melodic minor scale is like a major scale with just the 3rd scale degree flatted, or lowered, a half step. Converting a major scale to an ascending melodic minor scale requires the following scale degree formula: 1, 2, b3, 4, 5, 6, 7. Fortunately, the descending pattern is the same as the natural minor scale. Take a look at the next figure to see an ascending and descending C melodic minor scale.

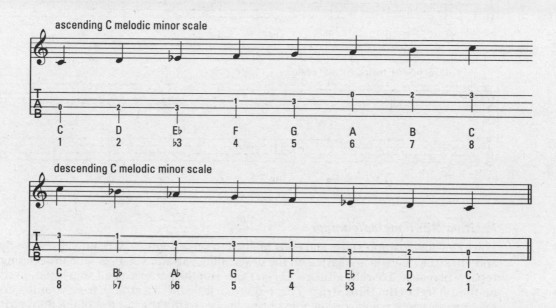

Composers in the Baroque and Classical music eras, like Bach, Handel and Mozart, often used the melodic minor scale to give their melodies an elaborate and complex sound. Nowadays, it's not to common to see the melodic minor scale outside of jazz improvisation (see Chapter 14 for improvising solos). Still though, for ukulele fingerstyle (see Chapter 9) it's important to have a good grasp of the melodic minor scale, because you never know when it will crop up in an old baroque or classical-style piece of music.

Position #1: F melodic minor

This first position of the F melodic minor scale starts and ends on the 5th scale degree – a 'C' note. The root note of the scale – the 'F' – falls on the 1st fret of the second string. Notice how on the descending pattern the 6th and 7th scale degrees – the 'D' and 'E' notes – are flatted. This turns the descending pattern into the natural minor scale.

Ascending pattern   Descending pattern

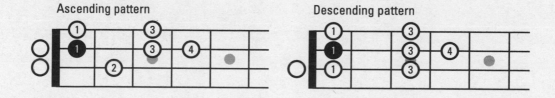

Track 211

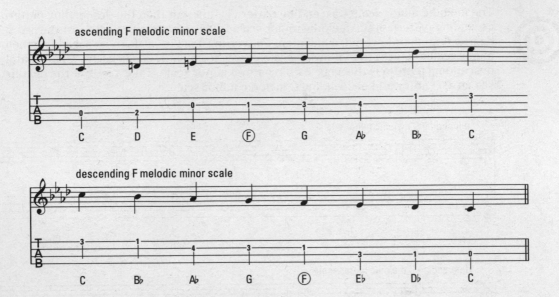

ascending F melodic minor scale

C D E Ⓕ G A♭ B♭ C

descending F melodic minor scale

C B♭ A♭ G Ⓕ E♭ D♭ C

Position #2: F melodic minor

The following position starts and ends on the 6th scale degree – a 'D' note. Because the 6th and 7th scale degrees are flatted on the descending pattern, you begin the descending pattern by playing a 'D♭' rather than a 'D'; you also end the pattern a half step lower on the 'D♭' on the 1st fret of the third string. This requires a little bit of a stretch from your fingers. You might experiment using your middle or ring fingers to fret the 3rd fret of the third string to see what it is easier.

Ascending pattern   Descending pattern

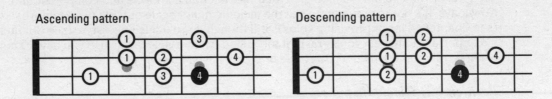

Track 212

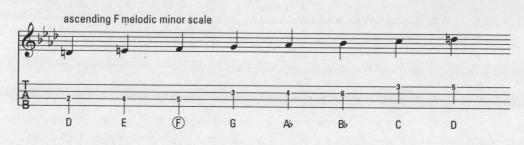

ascending F melodic minor scale

D E (F) G Ab Bb C D

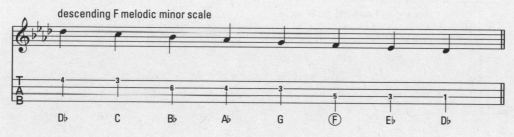

descending F melodic minor scale

Db C Bb Ab G (F) Eb Db

Position #3: F melodic minor

In this position, you get the truest sound of the F melodic minor scale because you're starting and ending on an 'F' – the strongest note of the scale.

Ascending pattern   Descending pattern

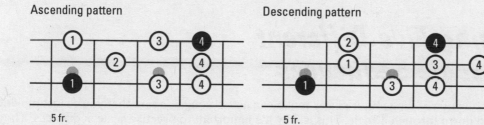

5 fr.   5 fr.

Track 213

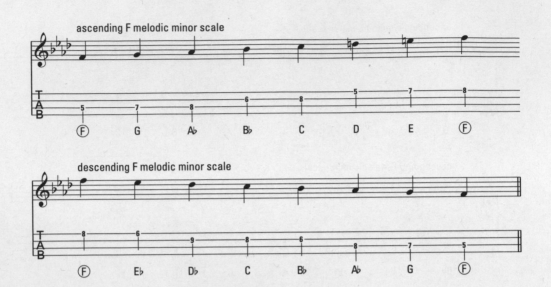

Slide this entire position up or down a couple of frets to play the melodic minor scale in another key. For example, if you shift this entire position down three frets, so the root notes of this position line up with the 'D' notes on the 2nd fret of the third string and the 5th fret of the first string, you would be playing a D melodic minor scale.

Practising Five Different Minor Scale Sequences

When you're using minor scales to play an actual song, it's rare that you're just moving up and down through a scale. This is why it's important to practise scale sequences. They get you used to anticipating different and even challenging movements in a melody.

Practise the following sequences at slow and fast tempos. In addition, you might practise these sequences at loud and soft volumes, but if you do, keep the notes as even in volume as possible throughout the entire sequence. Certain notes shouldn't be significantly louder or softer than other notes. Lastly, don't be afraid to slow these sequences down. Some of them can be a challenge, so don't rush things, and be patient with yourself.

You play this first sequence in D natural minor. Use position #1 of C natural minor and slide it up two frets to play in D minor. The trickiest part of this sequence is in the ascending pattern in the second measure where you're required to slide up your little finger to the 6th fret of the second string to accommodate the shift in the scale position. Likewise, in the descending pattern, in the last two measures, you need to shift the scale position down. Follow the numbers next to notes to see which fingers to use to fret certain notes.

Track 214

 The next sequence is played in C natural minor using position #1. The most challenging aspects to this sequence are the two finger jumps that happen in the ascending and descending sequence. To accommodate these jumps, you might use a finger to barre the strings. For example, in the ascending sequence, on the last note of the first measure and in the descending sequence, in the middle of the second measure, use your ring finger to press down on 3rd fret of the second and third strings.

Track 215

The following sequence is in E natural minor. Use position #1 of C natural minor, slide it up four frets, and you're playing E natural minor. Notice the finger jumps that happen in the ascending and descending patterns. Again, feel free to barre these strings. Also, check out the second to last notes of the ascending and descending sequences. These are out-of-position notes. In the ascending sequence, reach up with your little finger to play the 9th fret of the bottom string. In the descending sequence, reach down with your index finger to play the 2nd fret of the third string.

Track 216

For this next sequence, take position #3 of G harmonic minor and slide it down two frets to play in F harmonic minor. Since this position has a lot of stretches and finger jumps in it, this is a challenging sequence to get the feel for. Take this pattern a few notes at a time and pay close attention to the suggested fingerings. As you learn this pattern, try to memorise it; memorising allows you to get away from looking at the page and helps you to focus on what your fingers are doing.

Track 217

This last pattern sequence is in E melodic minor. Take position #3 of the F melodic minor scale and move it down one fret to make it E melodic minor.

Track 218

Playing Songs Using All Three Minor Scales

To really get a sense for how the three different minor scales sound and compare with one another, it's best to see how they sound and are used in actual songs.

Playing 'O Come, O Come Emmanuel'

To play 'O Come, O Come Emmanuel,' take position #1 of C natural minor and slide it up four frets to play in E minor. You'll notice there are some fret jumps that require you to get a little creative with your finger position. For these jumps, rather than barring the strings, try using a free finger to fret the adjacent string. Check out the fingering numbers in the next figure to see how this works.

O Come, O Come Emmanuel

Playing 'Coventry Carol'

'Coventry Carol' is a beautiful, almost haunting, Christmas carol written in G harmonic minor. The entire piece can be played in position #2. The only part of this song where the pattern breaks is the very last note. Instead of going to a flat 3rd scale degree – 'B*b*' – the 3rd scale degree is raised a half step to make it 'B'.

Coventry Carol

Playing 'Greensleeves'

One of the best examples of melodic minor is the beautiful song 'Greensleeves.' The song uses positions #2 and #3 of F melodic minor. You'll find that, when the song's melody descends, it follows the descending melodic minor pattern pretty closely (see measures 2–4, 10–12, 18–20, 26–28). In some parts, there are descending melodies that seem to follow more of the ascending melodic minor pattern, which seems like it's against the rules; but this is usually because there is an ascending melody that quickly follows and resolves back to the root note – 'F' (see measures 13–15, 29–31). In pieces of music that use the melodic minor scale, it's common for composers to break the rules a little bit to make the melody sound more interesting.

Chapter 13

Commanding the Fretboard with Chords

. . . .

In This Chapter

▶ Practising major and minor triads across the ukulele fretboard

▶ Using triads to play pieces of music

▶ Finding new ways to play chords in moveable positions

. . . .

In Chapter 11 and Chapter 12, you develop an understanding of the ukulele fretboard through major and minor scales. Scales, which are just a collection of individual notes, are essential because almost all songs are written around the notes of a scale to create a certain sound or feeling. Where the focus has previously been on the individual notes of a scale, in this chapter the attention turns towards seeing how you combine certain notes of a scale to build chords up and down the fretboard.

You build nearly all chords you play on the ukulele from a smaller three-note chord called a *triad*. Triads are the building blocks to the chords you play on the ukulele. If you know how to build a triad, you can discover new ways to play the same chord in several different places across the fretboard – without having to refer to a chord diagram! This adds variety to your playing and makes common chord progressions sound way more interesting. In addition, triads allow you to take a single-note melody line from a scale and add harmony around it to create a richer and fuller sound.

In this chapter, learn how to build two different types of triads up and down the ukulele fretboard. You take these triads and play two different songs. From there, take those triads and learn how to turn them into moveable chord positions that can be played in different positions across the fretboard to add variety to any song's chord progression. The following exercises help you further develop a mastery over the notes of the fretboard, and additionally, these exercises help build your chord vocabulary, develop independence between your fingers, improve your dexterity and strengthen your fretting hand.

Building Major and Minor Triads

A *triad* is just a fancy name for a chord made up of three notes. There are two very important triads: *major* and *minor*. From major and minor triads, you get major and minor chords. Makes sense. Each type of triad has its own distinct sound and mood, just like scales. The following exercises help build major and minor triads.

For each type of triad, I show you patterns and shapes that are used to play the triad in different places across the ukulele fretboard. Like scales, each triad has a root note. For example, a C major triad has the root note 'C', just as a B minor triad has the root note 'B'. In each triad diagram, the root note of the triad is represented by a black dot. If you know where the root note is located in each triad's position, you're able to move the entire triad position to make triads in other keys. I show you how to do this in a little bit.

For the purposes of demonstration, I teach you major and minor triads based on a 'G' root note. That means you will make G major and G minor triads. Practise playing and memorising each of these positions.

Constructing major triads

First, let's look at some basic theory for building a major triad.

 To build a major triad, take a major scale (see Chapter 11) and sound the 1st, 3rd and 5th scale degrees at the same time. For example, to build a G major triad, take a G major scale and identify the 1st, 3rd and 5th notes in the scale, as shown in the following figure.

Based on the major scale, the formula for building a major triad is **1-3-5**. In this example, a G major triad is spelled G-B-D.

To play a G major triad on the ukulele, you're required to simultaneously sound the 'G', 'B' and 'D' notes. To do this, you must play each of these notes on a separate string. Since there are three notes in a triad, play the G major triad across the bottom three strings of the ukulele, as shown in the following figures.

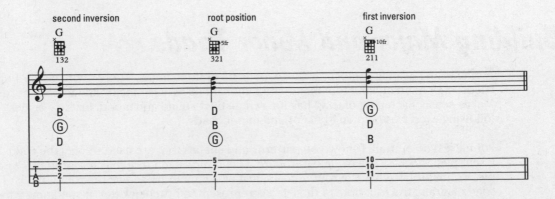

For each of the three positions, the notes of the triad are arranged into different *inversions*. In root position, the 'G' note (1st scale degree or *root note*) is the lowest note of the triad. In first inversion, the 'B' (3rd scale degree) is the lowest note of the triad. In second inversion, the 'D' (5th scale degree) is the lowest note of the triad. Each of these positions is a G major chord, but as you can hear, each inversion has a different tone and texture when played, which is perfect for adding variation to a song's chord progression.

As you practise these G major triad positions, memorise where the root note is located in each position (represented by a black dot). This allows you to create major triads in other keys. For example, take a G major triad in *root position* and slide down the entire position two frets. By doing this, you create an F major triad in root position. This is because the root note of the position is lined up with the 'F' note on the 5th fret of the C-string. Likewise, if you were to take the *second inversion* G major triad and slide it up two frets, you would be playing an A major triad in second inversion because the root note in second inversion is lined up with the 'A' note on the 5th fret of the E-string. Take this same idea and play major triads in other keys.

Depending on the size of your ukulele and fingers, some of the inversions played higher on the fretboard are near impossible to play. Try your best to play these higher inversions. Adjust your fingers as much as possible to ensure that every string rings out clearly and in tune. If there just isn't any space for your fingers, it's okay. Still though, learn these triad positions because these positions can be used lower on the fretboard to play major triads in other keys.

Putting together minor triads

Like major and minor scales, major triads are often felt as happy and cheerful, whereas minor triads are often felt as sad and melancholy. To build a minor triad, take a major triad and flat the 3rd scale degree (lower it a half step; move it down one fret). For example, in a G major triad, you have notes G-B-D. To make this into a minor triad, flat the 3rd – the 'B' – to make the triad G-B♭-D. Based on a major scale, the formula for building a minor triad is **1-b3-5**.

Another way to see it is that a minor triad is constructed from the 1st, 3rd and 5th scale degrees of a minor scale (see Chapter 12). The following figure takes a G minor scale and circles the 1st, 3rd and 5th scale degrees to indicate which notes form a G minor triad.

The following figures show three different G minor triad inversions across the ukulele fretboard. Take time to pay attention to where the root note in each inversion is located (represented by a black dot), so you can slide these positions around to form minor triads in other keys.

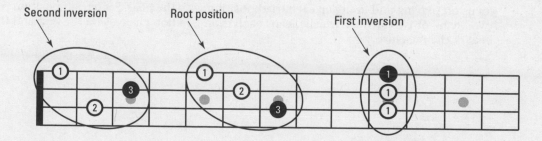

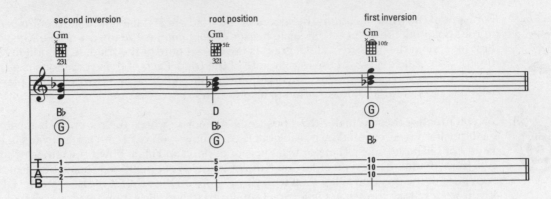

 The trickiest position is the first inversion minor triad. To make things easier, use your index finger to barre the bottom three strings for this position. Just ensure that your thumb is firmly planted on the neck of the ukulele to help get the necessary pressure against the strings so they ring out clearly.

 Practise moving these positions up and down the fretboard to form other minor triads. For example, if you move the root position G minor triad down three frets, you play an E minor triad, because the root note of the root position minor triad is lined up with the 'E' note on the 4th fret of the C-string. If you move the first inversion G minor triad down five frets, you play a D minor triad, because the root note of the first inversion minor triad position is lined up with the 'D' note on the 5th fret of the A-string. Likewise, if you move the second inversion G minor triad up four frets, you play a B minor triad, because the root note of the second inversion minor triad position is lined up with the 'B' note on the 7th fret of the E-string. If you are still learning the notes of the fretboard, again, be sure to refer to the Cheat Sheet to find notes across the fretboard.

Practising Triads Up and Down the Fretboard

The following exercises require you to think on your feet and anticipate changes between different triad positions. It's one thing to know how to play a triad; it's another thing to use triads in a musical way. These exercises sharpen your ability to change chords, show you how to form different types of triads in other keys, challenge your brain power and bring you towards playing actual songs with triads.

 These exercises are both physical and mental. Your ability to play these exercises smoothly is dependent upon your physical ability to move and change your fingers into different positions. In addition, playing these exercises smoothly is dependent upon memorising the location of a triad's root note, so you can anticipate the chord changes. It takes time and repetition for your fingers to build up muscle memory and for your mind to remember where the root notes are located, so be patient with yourself and take it slow.

For each exercise, play at a very slow tempo (40–60 BPM, if you have a metronome) and focus on playing and lining up each triad position with the beat. Each triad position receives two beats, or two strums, which means each triad position changes on the first and third beat of the measure.

Major triad exercises

Major chords are used all the time in songs. To be ready for anything, practise major triads in all different positions across the fretboard, while forming major triads in different keys.

For each of these exercises, either strum down or pluck the bottom three strings with your fingers – whatever is most comfortable for you. Make it your goal to play every exercise as cleanly as possible, so every note rings out. Try your best to avoid sounding the top g-string.

In this first exercise, practise switching between D, G and A major triads in root position. Throughout the exercise, maintain the same finger position, just slide the position up an down to each chord.

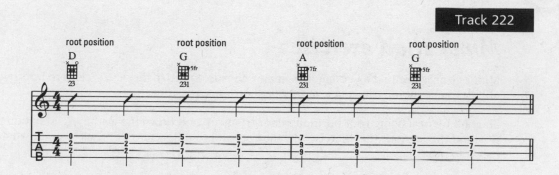

For this next exercise, practise switching between Bb and Eb major triads, while cycling between all three triad inversions. For each chord, start each triad at the root position, proceed to the first inversion, second inversion and then back to the root position.

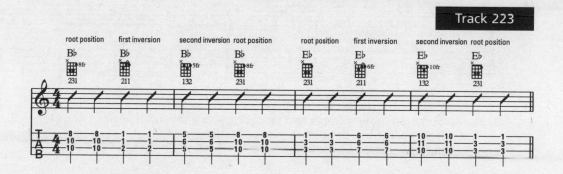

Practise changing between F and Bb major triads, however, this time, switch things up and start each triad in second inversion, proceed to the first inversion, root position and then back to second inversion.

Track 224

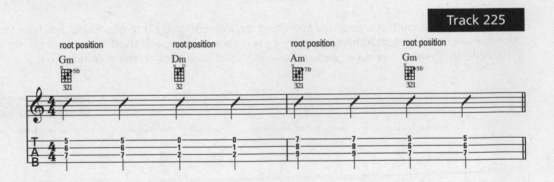

Write out your own chord progressions in your practice journal and practise cycling through the different triad inversions for each chord, as you did in these exercises.

Minor triad exercises

Minor chords are just as common as major chords. Practise these exercises to improve your ability to use minor triads in a variety of chord progressions.

Start off by practising root position minor triads up and down the fretboard. Maintain the position throughout the exercise but slide around to different root notes to create minor triads in other keys.

Track 225

Take two common minor chords and practise cycling through the inversions for each chord up and down the fretboard. Begin in root position, move to first inversion, second inversion and then back to root position.

Track 226

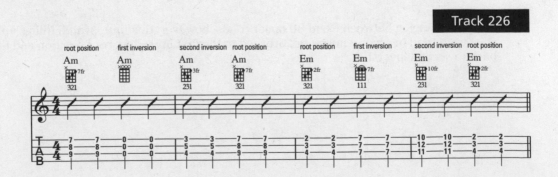

This time cycle through each minor triad inversion starting in second inversion, moving to first inversion, root position and then, back to second inversion.

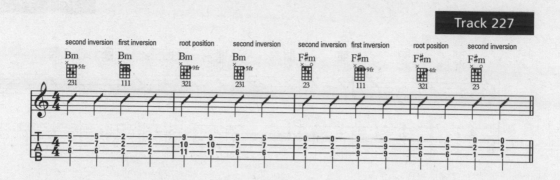

Combined triad exercises

Kick it up a notch and practise switching between major and minor triads in different inversions across the fretboard. In actual songs, it's normal to play different types of chords throughout the song, so these exercises stretch your ability to think about multiple triad positions in all different types of keys. Before playing each exercise, take the time to look at what notes are being used and how they're being played across the fretboard.

Play a common major and minor chord progression using just triads. For the first time through the progression, play all triads in root position, then proceed to cycle through the progression in first inversion, second inversion and lastly, back again in root position.

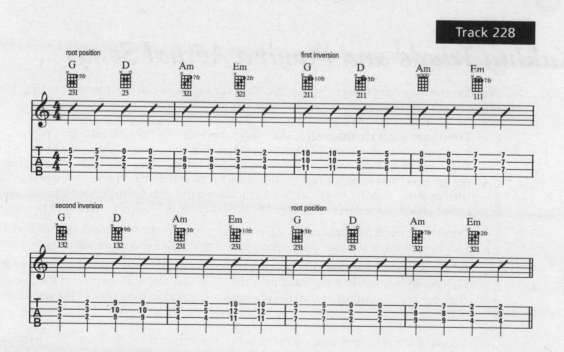

As in the last exercise, combine major and minor triads over a common chord progression.

Track 229

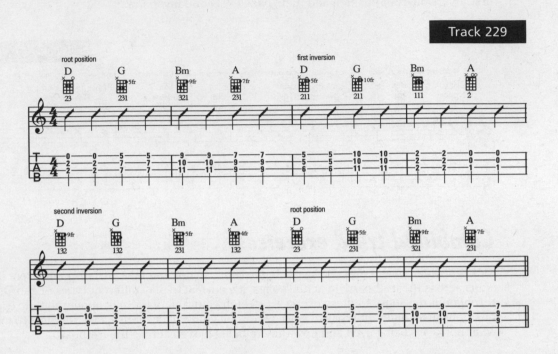

To continue your practice, take your own chord progression using major and minor chords, find the different triad positions for each chord, and practise playing through the progression using only triads, just like you did for the previous two exercises.

Taking Triads and Playing Actual Songs

Practise the following songs to get some ideas for how you can use triads in a song. Most often, triads are used in three main ways:

✔ **Triads are used rhythmically.** Most songs have a chord progression that repeats multiple times through a song. For certain parts of the song, you might take a chord's triad and strum it in a different inversion on the fretboard. Doing this takes the simplest chord progression and makes it more interesting for your listener. In addition, if you're playing with another ukulele player, rather than playing the exact same chord shapes, use a different chord inversion to complement the other ukulele player and fill out the sound.

✔ **Triads are used harmonically.** With triads, you can take a single-note melody line and harmonise notes to make the melody line sound fuller and more intricate.

✔ **Triads are used melodically.** Say you are trying to discover the melody line of a song across the fretboard. If the song uses the chords C major, G major and F major, chances are, the notes of the melody lines are found in the notes of the triad for each of these chords, or at least, close to the notes of the triad.

Take a look at the next two songs to see how triads are used to create rhythm, harmony and melody. The first song is based around a single-note melody line, but triads are added in to create beautiful harmonies. The second song's melody is carried along with a full-bodied, driving rhythm through the use of triads.

Playing 'Red River Valley'

The tender song 'Red River Valley' is an old cowboy tune. The melody of the song is so well written that it stands on its own, but by using triads to harmonise certain notes, you're able to add a little bit more character to the song and fill out the sound.

Throughout the song, triads are strummed on the first beat of some measures. The most common triad used in the song is the F major triad played on the bottom three strings in second inversion. The squiggly line next to these triads indicates that you should strum through these notes.

There are a couple of areas worth paying more attention to. You'll notice in measures 3 and 10 that the 'F' and 'C' notes are combined to form a two-note chord. These are the bottom two notes of the F major triad in second inversion. The reason a triad isn't played in these spots is to ensure that the melody of the song is the highest sounding note. Keeping the melody as the highest note allows it to standout from the other notes. In addition, take a look at measure 11. The triad that is strummed on beat one of the measure is like a first inversion B♭ triad, but it has a 'C' note as the top note, rather than a 'B♭'. This creates a little bit of tension that quickly resolves by sounding into a B♭ major triad on the second beat of the measure.

Play 'Red River Valley' with a soft, tender feel, and try to make all of the notes ring out as evenly and clearly as possible. To pluck the strings, use your thumb, index or middle fingers.

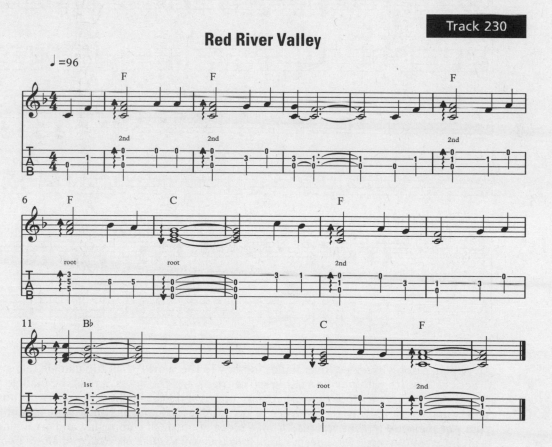

Playing 'Joy to the World'

In this arrangement of 'Joy to the World,' use major triads to harmonise the melody of the song. All of the major triad positions are played in an inversion that puts the melody line of the song as the highest note of the triad. This allows the melody of the song to really stand out against the other notes.

About halfway through the song, at measure 8 and 9, the harmony drops out to just the melody line of the song. For this part, you can use F major scale position #3 from Chapter 11. Dropping out to just the melody and coming back in with triads in measure 13 creates a nice dynamic that breaks up the song.

 Take this song slow at first and learn it just a little bit at a time. This song really stretches your ability to jump between triad positions up and down the fretboard, but once you get it down, you feel like a million bucks. You'll find that the more time you spend memorising the song the easier it is to focus on moving your fingers to hit the right notes.

Joy to the World

Track 231

 Arranging a song like 'Red River Valley' or 'Joy to the World' to fit the ukulele takes a lot of practice. It starts with having a fair grasp of triads and the notes across the ukulele fretboard. As you spend more time practising scales and learning how the notes of those scales make chords with triads, you can start to try harmonising single note melodies that your ear picks up or that you read from a piece of music. If composing and arranging songs is an interest of yours, for a deeper look into this world, pick up a copy of *Music Composition For Dummies* by Scott Jarrett and Holly Day (Wiley).

Turning Triads Into Moveable Chord Positions

A moveable chord is one where a finger is fretting each of the four strings of the ukulele. Unlike a triad, which covers only three strings, moveable chords are based around triads but allow you to strum all four strings to create a fuller and richer sound.

Take a major or minor triad and make it into a moveable chord by doubling the note from the bottom A-string of the triad on the top g-string. In this way, there is a finger fretting each string of the ukulele, which makes it a moveable chord position. The chord is moveable in that, since all four strings are fretted, you can easily move the position up and down the fretboard to play chords in other keys, much like you did for triads. In the following examples and exercises, I show you how to do this.

Moveable chord positions are beneficial to use in songs because they add variety. Rather than playing the same chord the same way over and over again, play it in a different position on the fretboard to create interest for your listener. Likewise, if you are playing with another ukulele player, rather than playing the chords the same exact way, use different moveable positions to open things up and make the overall sound more dynamic.

Making moveable major chords

The following figure shows G major triads turned into moveable chord positions. Notice how the notes on the bottom three strings arc just like the G major triad positions you learned earlier in this chapter. Take time to practise the different finger positions while strumming through each chord.

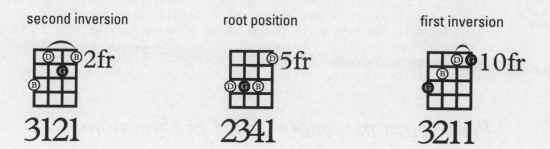

second inversion   root position   first inversion

The root position chord is the hardest to perform. The fingering above is the most common suggested fingering for this chord, however, if you have large fingers like me, it can be hard to squeeze your fingers into that position. In this way, for this position, I like to place my index finger on the 5th fret of the bottom string and use my ring finger to barre the top three strings on the 7th fret. While doing this, I ensure that my ring finger is bent up and out a little bit to avoid touching or muting the bottom string. Experiment with both ways and see what position is most comfortable for you.

Moveable positions require the use of more fingers, which means there is a higher probability that a certain note won't ring out in the chord. If you notice a note isn't ringing out or if you hear a buzzing sound, try readjusting your fingers and adding more pressure to the strings. Take time to pluck each individual string in the chord to ensure that each note rings out clearly. By doing so, you can isolate the problematic notes and find the best position.

Move these major chord positions up and down the fretboard to play major chords in other keys. For example, if you take the moveable G major chord position based on a second inversion triad and move it up two frets, you are playing an A major chord. This is because the root note of the chord (represented by a black dot) is lined up with the 'A' note on the 5th fret of the E-string. Take this same idea to come up with other major chords in different positions across the ukulele fretboard.

Assembling moveable minor chords

Next, take G minor triads and make them into moveable chord positions, as shown in the following figure. Be sure to practise moving these positions around the fretboard to come up with minor chords in other keys.

second inversion   root position   first inversion

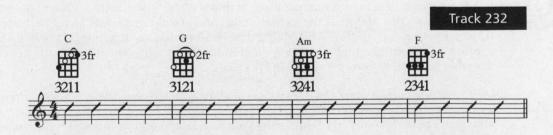

3241   3421   3111

The G minor chord based on a first inversion triad is a tough one to manage because of how cramped the 10th to 12th frets get on the ukulele. In the context of playing a G minor chord in an actual song, it's best to use one of the other positions lower down the fretboard. At the same time, you can still use the minor chord based on the first inversion triad to play minor chords in other keys at a lower spot on the fretboard. For example, if you take the G minor chord based on the first inversion triad and move it down seven frets, you are playing a C minor chord, because the root note of the position is lined up with the 'C' note on the 3rd fret of the bottom A-string and the 'C' note on the 5th fret of the top g-string.

Practising moveable chord progressions

Take the two following common chord progressions and use moveable chord positions. Don't forget to write out and come up with your own chord progressions too!

Track 232

Track 233

Notice in the previous chord progressions that chord positions are selected so that they are located close by each other. For example, in the first chord progression, each chord uses a position that finds itself between the 2nd and 5th frets. You might practise using other positions for this chord progression, but in actual songs, locate chord positions nearby each other so you can more quickly switch between chords.

Getting Jazzy with Moveable Seventh Chords

Major and minor chords are some of the most common chords. Seventh chords are built around major and minor triads, but they have an added note that gives them a jazzier sound. In the following examples and exercises, you build seventh chords of different types and then practise playing a couple of popular jazz chord progressions.

Figuring out dominant seventh chords

A *dominant seventh* chord is a chord written like: G7, C7, A7, and so on. These chords find themselves in all sorts of songs, from simple folk music to elaborate classical compositions.

To build a dominant seventh chord, take a major triad and add a flatted 7th note from the root note of the chord's major scale. For example, to build a G7, take a G major scale. Circle the notes of the major triad (G-B-D), and then lower the 7th scale degree a half step from F sharp to F natural. The following figure shows exactly this.

Normally, in a G major scale, the 'F' note is an 'F#' note. However, to build a dominant seventh chord, you flat the seventh scale degree (lower the note a half step). In this way, the dominant seventh chord formula based on a major scale is: **1-3-5-b7**. This means a G7 chord uses the notes G-B-D-F.

Because there are four different notes in a seventh chord, each of these notes must be played on one of the four strings of the ukulele. The following figure shows a variety of different ways to play G7 chord across the ukulele fretboard. The root note in the chord 'G' is represented by a black dot.

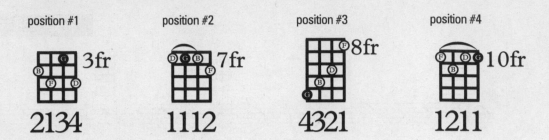

position #1   position #2   position #3   position #4

The higher you go up the fretboard, the harder it is to fret those notes. Each of these positions is moveable in that you can move them up and down the fretboard to create other dominant seventh chords. If one position is too difficult to play, still learn it, but move it down the fretboard to create a dominant seventh chord in a different key. For example, to play an C7 chord, move down position #4 of the G7 chord seven frets to line up the root note in the chord with the 'C' note on the 3rd fret of the bottom A-string.

Mastering major seventh chords

The next moveable seventh chord you learn is the *major seventh* chord. Major seventh chords are typically written like: Cmaj7, Dmaj7, Gmaj7, etc.

A major seventh chord is built from the 1st, 3rd, 5th and 7th scale degrees of a major scale. In this way, the major seventh chord formula based on a major scale is: **1-3-5-7**. To build a Gmaj7 chord, use the G major scale and circle those notes, as shown in the following figure.

As you can see the major seventh chord differentiates itself from a dominant seventh chord in that the seventh scale degree is *not* lowered a half step.

Now, practise the four different moveable major seventh chord positions using a Gmaj7 chord. If the third and fourth positions are too difficult to fret that high on the fretboard, practise them lower on the fretboard to form a major seventh chord in a different key. Continue to pay attention to where the root note is located in the chord so you can move the position to create major seventh chords in other keys.

position #1   position #2   position #3   position #4

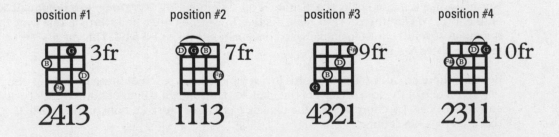

Tackling minor seventh chords

To build a minor seventh chord, take a dominant seventh chord and lower the 3rd degree a half step. So the formula to build a minor seventh chord based on a major scale is: **1-b3-5-b7**. Minor seventh chords are typically written: Cm7, Dmin7, Gm7, etc.

Check out the following figure to see the minor seventh formula applied to a G major scale to build a Gm7 chord. As you can see, the 3rd and 7th scale degrees are flatted.

Take a look at four different moveable minor seventh chord positions using a Gm7 chord.

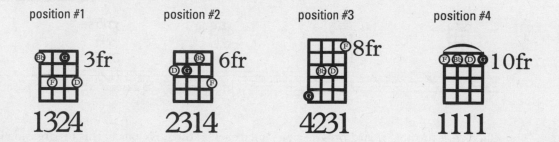

position #1   position #2   position #3   position #4

 Avoid using the third position to play a minor seventh chord. While it is an option, and worth mentioning, the amount of strength and stretching required to execute the chord cleanly makes the other positions much more appealing. Definitely practise it, as it can help stretch and strengthen your fingers, but in the context of an actual song, opt for one of the other positions.

Practising jazz chord progressions

Seventh chords are the bread and butter to jazz music. Practise the following three jazz chord progressions to work out your fingers and practise moveable seventh chord positions in a variety of different keys. These chord progressions challenge your ability to switch chords smoothly and help strengthen your fingers.

 If you're unable to change chords and keep steady timing, don't be afraid to slow down the tempo and practise changing chords separate from strumming.

The first chord progression you practise is the most popular jazz chord progression of all time: the ii-V-I progression. Jazz chord progressions are typically represented by roman numerals, a theoretical way to represent the relationships between chords in a song. So a ii-V-I chord progression is said 'two five one.' Jazz legends like Django Reinhardt, Pat Martino and Charlie Parker use a ii-V-I progression as a staple in their music. In fact, the jazz solos you pick up in Chapter 14 use a ii-V-I progression.

In the following exercise, try your hand at a ii-V-I progression in the key of D. The first chord is strumming over four beats, the second chord over four beats and the last chord over eight beats, since it is played over two measures. Just use simple down strums as you practise.

The following jazz chord progression uses four different chords that each receive four beats.

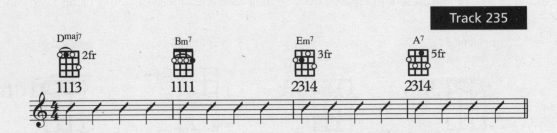

Check out the next chord progression. Since each of the positions in this progression is played using a barre chord, use your index finger as a constant barre shape that slides up and down the fretboard to smoothly navigate between these chord positions.

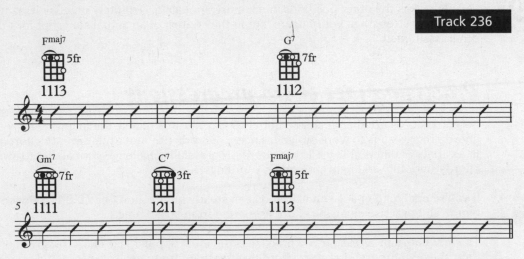

TIP

To continue practising moveable seventh chord positions, take the previous chord progressions and try to play those chords in other positions across the ukulele fretboard.

Chapter 14

Using Scales to Solo and Improvise

In This Chapter

▶ Learning how to use scales to improvise solos

▶ Practising licks and riffs

▶ Crafting rock, blues and jazz solos

To improvise a solo on the ukulele, you don't just play random notes on the spot, but rather, you take your knowledge of different scales and piece it all together in a musical way. In order to do this, you have to build a vocabulary of *licks* or *riffs*. A lick is a just short collection of notes played over a couple of measures.

In this chapter, I show you how to solo in three popular genres of music: rock, blues and jazz. Each genre uses a different scale to create a rock sound, a soulful bluesy sound, or a complex jazzy sound. For each scale, you learn different licks and how to use these to create a solo over common chord progressions. Some of the licks incorporate hammer-ons, pull-offs, slides and bends, so if these are new techniques for you, head over to Chapter 10 to work through exercises that help you improve these techniques.

In each section of this chapter, a different scale is presented in a variety of positions across the fretboard. As a practice exercise, ascend and descend through each scale pattern presented, and while you're doing that, focus on playing each note of the scale as cleanly and evenly as possible. For the exercises, break up the licks into small sections and keep things slow at first. For example, you might only learn a measure of the lick at a time. When you're comfortable, use the backing tracks from the audio examples associated with each section to practise applying the licks. And most of all, be sure to experiment and come up with your own licks and solos – that's what makes improvising solos so fun!

Note: You won't find figures for audio Tracks 237, 244, 249 or 251 in this chapter. They are backing tracks, against which you can practise licks and solos.

Rocking Out with Pentatonic Scales

The pentatonic scale comes in two different flavours: minor and major. In any pentatonic scale, there are only five notes. For soloing, the pentatonic scale is a must-know because of how diverse it is and how simple it is to implement into a chord progression. This scale is commonly used in rock, blues, country and jazz.

Learning the minor pentatonic scale

The minor pentatonic scale is built from the 1st, 3rd, 4th, 5th and 7th scale degrees of the natural minor scale (see Chapter 12 to learn about the natural minor scale). Use this scale make a solo sound darker and moodier. Take a look at the following figures to see how to build and play an F minor pentatonic scale.

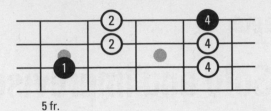

5 fr.

F   Ab   Bb   C   Eb   F

Take this scale pattern and move it up and down across the fretboard to play the minor pentatonic scale in other keys. For example, if you move the entire scale pattern down three frets, you're playing a D minor pentatonic scale, as shown in the following figure. This is because the root note of the pattern (represented by the black dot) is lined up with a D note on the 2nd fret of the third string.

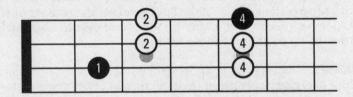

For now, focus on learning the F minor pentatonic scale up and down the fretboard. You will use the F minor pentatonic scale to solo in the upcoming exercises. Take a look at the following figure to see the scale played in multiple positions across the fretboard.

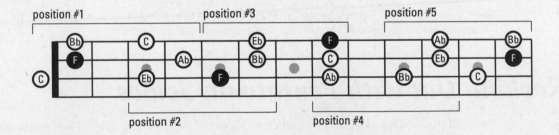

Constructing the major pentatonic scale

The major pentatonic scale is built from the 1st, 2nd, 3rd, 5th and 6th scale degrees of the major scale (see Chapter 11 to learn about the major scale). Unlike the minor pentatonic, major pentatonic has a sweeter, smoother sound to it. Check out the following figure to build an F major pentatonic scale.

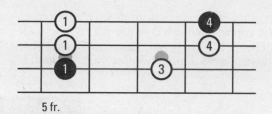

5 fr.

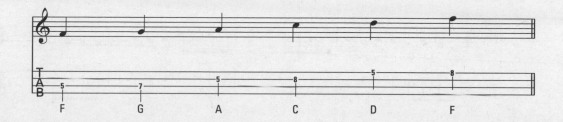

F   G   A   C   D   F

Turn any minor pentatonic scale pattern into major pentatonic by looking at the minor pentatonic scale's relative major (see section 'Harnessing the power of relative minor and major' in Chapter 12). For example, D minor is relative to F major. This means a D minor pentatonic scale pattern shape, such as the one earlier in this chapter, can be used to solo in F major pentatonic because it uses the same notes as the F major pentatonic scale.

In the following figure, see the different positions of the F major pentatonic scale played across the fretboard.

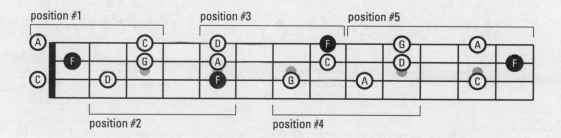

Practising pentatonic scale licks and exercises

It's time to put the minor and major pentatonic scales into action. Use the F-E♭-B♭ chord progression backing track, Track 237, to practise the following pentatonic scale licks and exercises. In this first sequence, the F minor pentatonic scale is played over a simple chord progression in the key of F major. The F minor pentatonic scale contrasts over the major key to create a darker, more colourful sound.

Track 238

Take the same chord progression, but move the scale pattern down three frets to make the pattern F major pentatonic. Essentially, you're playing a D minor pentatonic scale pattern, but since D minor is relative to F major, over this particular chord progression, the scale pattern sounds in F major pentatonic. This produces a nice, sweeter, buttery sound.

Track 239

To craft a great solo, you don't need to try to cram every note of the scale into every measure of the song. You might repeat a note over and over again, or you might make certain notes longer or shorter to create tension and draw your listener into the solo. The following exercise uses the minor pentatonic scale.

Track 240

Sliding between notes in a scale is a great way to make your solo ebb and flow. In the following exercise, the first note of the measure slides up from the 3rd fret to the 5th fret on the second string. Use your ring finger to perform this slide because you want your index finger freed up to play the 3rd fret of the bottom string. Be sure to listen to the audio for this exercise because this exercise looks harder than it sounds.

The next exercise incorporates the use of pull-offs and slides to inject emotion and feeling into the lick. For the pull-offs that happen in the first measure, use your index finger to barre the bottom two strings on the 8th fret to minimize movement and increase fluidity. For the slide that happens on the first beat of the second measure, use your ring finger to slide up from the 6th fret to the 8th fret on the second string. This keeps your middle and index fingers freed up to descend through the scale in the following beats.

Track 242

Playing a rock solo

By now, you have some licks under your belt that can applied, modified and varied to improvise a rock solo. When you improvise, you pull from what you know and put it together in a way that tells a story. In the following exercise, use a major pentatonic scale to solo.

Don't try to rush through the solo. As you learn it, take it section by section. Count out loud slowly at first to sense how the notes in each section fall within the chord progression. In addition, listen to the solo in the audio track as much as possible to hear and sense how the solo fits within the progression.

Track 243

Expressing Soul with the Blues Scale

As a genre, blues is so distinctive that it has its own scale named after it. To make any solo sound bluesy, you have to know how to use the blues scale. Use the D7-G7 chord progression backing track, Track 244, to practise the following exercises.

Building the blues scale

The blues scale is like the minor pentatonic scale with just one added note between the 3rd and 4th scale degrees, as shown in the following figure. This additional note is often referred to as the 'blue note' because, as you'll see, when you play the blue note, it instantly makes any lick sound like the blues. The following figures show a D blues scale.

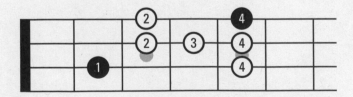

Take this scale pattern and move it around the fretboard to play a blues scale in other keys. In the following figure, the blues scale pattern is moved up two frets to play an E blues scale.

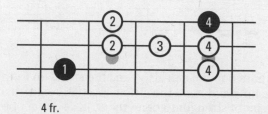

4 fr.

Just focus on the D blues scale for now. Check out the following figure to see how the D blues scale is played across the fretboard in different positions.

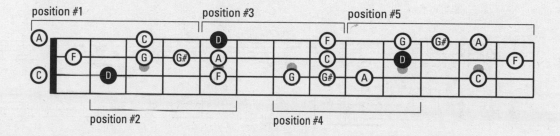

Practising blues scale licks and exercises

Since the blues scale is closely related to the minor pentatonic scale, the licks you know for the minor pentatonic scale sound great over a blues-style chord progression. The following exercises and licks make use of the added blue note. And because this is the blues, don't forget to swing the beat.

Part of being able to craft a solo is being able to navigate smoothly through a scale. This first exercise gets your fingers moving with a D blues scale sequence played over a simple chord progression.

Track 245

An effective blues soloing technique is to quickly slide up and down from the blue note in a chord progression. This really gives the solo that blues sound. Check out the following exercise to get a feel for it.

Track 246

Not only can you slide up from a blue note but you can also bend the string up from the blue note. This means you start on the blue note and bend the string up a half step to match the pitch of the note one fret up. It takes a bit of strength to bend the string, so don't be afraid to use multiple fingers.

Track 247

In this next exercise, use hammer-ons and pull-offs to transition to and from the blue note.

Track 248

Playing a blues solo

Try your hand at playing a solo over the 12 bar blues in D. In the following figure, for the first four measures, you're in the normal D blues scale position. In measures 4 to 8, switch to a higher position on the fretboard. Then, in the last four measures, return to the starting D blues scale position. Use the 12 bar blues backing track, Track 249, to practise the solo.

Track 250

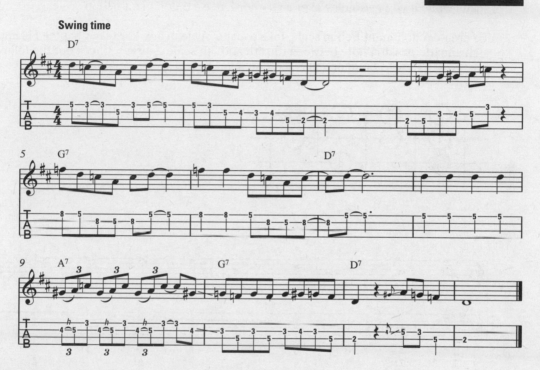

Sounding Jazzy with the Bebop Scale

As a genre of music, jazz can be a bit of a brain-buster because the scale you use to craft a solo often depends on what chord you're playing. In this way, soloing in jazz isn't like the rock or blues where it almost always sounds great to play any note from the pentatonic scale over an entire chord progression.

To improvise a jazz solo, it's all about tastefully inserting chromatic notes. A *chromatic note* is one that isn't included in the prevailing scale of the song. These chromatic notes outside the scale create *dissonance*. This is just a fancy word to refer to a combination of notes that sound harsh, displeasing and unresolved. When the chromatic notes return to notes inside the scale, there is a sense of resolution and stability, which is called *consonance*. Too much dissonance can sound jarring and hard to listen to, whereas if there is too much consonance, everything can start to sound boring. Creating a great jazz solo is all about balancing between dissonance and consonance to create interest for your listener.

In the bebop scale, chromatic notes are built into the scale to give it that jazzy sound. There are a few different types of bebop scales. Two of the most common are dominant and major bebop scales.

Discovering the dominant bebop scale

The dominant bebop scale sounds the best when played over dominant 7th chords like: G7, C7, D7, E7, A7, and so on. For example, to solo over a G7 chord, use a G dominant bebop scale, while if you're soloing over a C7 chord, use a C dominant bebop scale.

To create a dominant bebop scale, take a major scale in any key (see Chapter 11) and add in a chromatic passing note between the 6th and 7th scale degrees. Check out the following figures to see how to build and play a G dominant bebop scale.

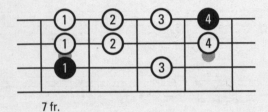

7 fr.

Move this scale pattern to play in other keys. For example, if you move the scale position down five frets, you're playing a D dominant bebop scale, as shown in the following figure.

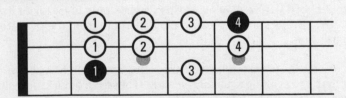

For now, just focus on the G dominant bebop scale. Take a look at the following figure to see how a G dominant bebop scale is played over the entire fretboard. Practise familiarising yourself with these other positions because you use these in the upcoming exercises.

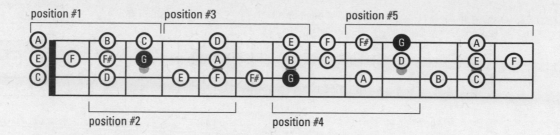

Mastering the major bebop scale

Where a dominant bebop scale works best over dominant 7th chords, the major bebop scale is often used over major 7th chords like Cmaj7, Gmaj7, Dmaj7, Amaj7, and so on.

To build a major bebop scale, take a major scale in any key and insert a chromatic passing note between the 5th and 6th scale degrees. The following figures show how to build and play a C major bebop scale.

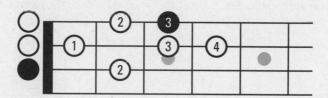

Use this scale to play in any other key by moving the entire scale pattern up the fretboard. For example, move the scale pattern up two frets and you're playing the D major bebop scale, as shown in the following figure. For the 'Ab' note that falls on the 6th fret of the second string, slide up your little finger from the preceding note in the pattern.

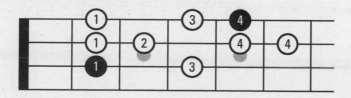

For now, just focus on learning the C major bebop scale, because you use this scale in the following exercises. The following figure shows the C major bebop scale played in multiple positions across the ukulele fretboard.

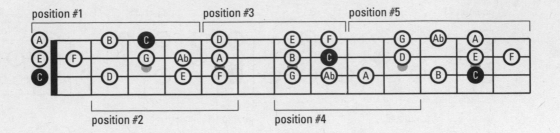

Practising bebop scale licks and exercises

Take the dominant and major bebop scales to craft and improvise solos. To do this, build a vocabulary of bebop scale licks. As you practise and familiarise yourself with these licks, modify them to create your own.

Practise the following licks over what's called a ii-V-I progression (said 'two five one progression'). This is an extremely common type of jazz chord progression. In the key of C, the chords are Dm7, G7 and Cmaj7, as shown in the following figure. For the ii and V chords–Dm7 and G7–use the dominant bebop scale to solo. For the I chord – Cmaj7 – use the major bebop scale to solo.

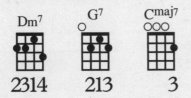

Check out the following exercise. In the first measure, you play an ascending G dominant bebop scale starting on a 'D' note. To create a bit more interest in the melody, create some variation by skipping around and going up and down through the scale, as shown in measure two. For measure three, switch to using the notes in a C major bebop scale. Use the Dm7-G7-Cmaj7 jazz progression backing track, Track 251, to practise the following jazz licks, solos and exercises.

Track 252

Swing time

Rather than playing one continuous sequence of notes, try resting for certain beats and holding certain notes longer than others. Here's a classic bebop lick that can be played in two octaves. In the higher octave, make use of your little finger to reach for those higher notes.

Track 253

Playing in a triplet rhythm is another way to create more interesting jazz solos. In the following exercise, use a triplet on the first beat of the second measure. Be sure to count this out loud at a slow tempo first to get a feel for it. Notice there are some finger jumps in the first two measures. Don't hesitate to use your index finger to barre the strings to jump between these notes.

Track 254

A great way to make a melody line sound even more jazzy is to use a technique called *enclosure*. To perform an enclosure, take a target note, such as the root note of the scale, play a note one fret above the target note, then play a note one fret below the target note, and then play the target note. In the following exercise, an enclosure happens on the first three notes of the second measure, with a high 'G' root note being targeted.

Track 255

Playing a jazz solo

In this last exercise, practise soloing over a twelve bar ii-V-I jazz progression. Use the backing track from the audio examples to improvise your own solos. If you're still looking for more ways to improve your soloing, try these couple of tips:

- ✔ **Start the solo on a note found in the chord you are soloing over.** For example, take a Dm7 chord. Since it's a minor chord, it's built upon a minor triad with the notes D-F-A (see Chapter 13 for building triads). As you'll notice, in all of the exercises, the first note played over a Dm7 chord is a D, F, or A note.

- ✔ **Place chromatic notes on the offbeat.** While enclosures are an exception to this, as a rule of thumb, don't always play chromatic notes, or notes outside of the scale, right on the counts of one, two, three, or four. Play these notes on the 'and' of these beats. This allows you to provide colour to the melody while still establishing a sense of stability and resolution to it because the notes of the scale are being played on strong beats.

- ✔ **Use triads to outline a melody line.** If you're not sure what to play, you might use your knowledge of triads from Chapter 13 to find notes that fit over a certain chord. For example, a G7 chord is built upon a G major triad with the notes G-B-D. Over a G7 chord, you might centre your solo around these three notes and then add other notes around these notes to add colour to the melody.

With jazz, rules are meant to be broken. The best way to approach solos is to experiment. Every now and then, you might surprise yourself by what you come up with. If you're interested in learning more about how to build chords and use different scales, check out *Music Theory for Dummies, 2nd Edition* by Holly Day and Michael Pilhofer (Wiley).

In a jazz solo, it's common to have to switch between different scale positions. Pay attention to the finger numbers above certain notes to give you a hint for how to play certain passages in this solo. Again, take it section by section and start slow.

Track 256

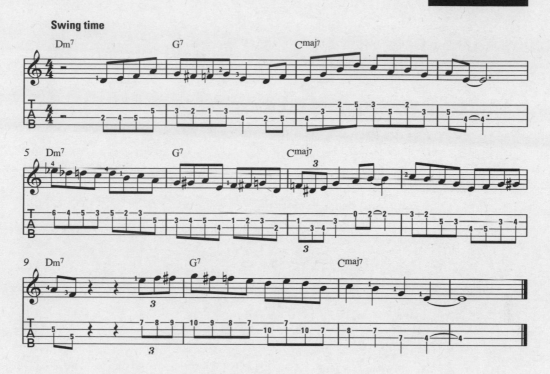

Part V
The Part of Tens

Go to www.dummies.com/go/ukuleleexercises to listen to ukulele audio tracks.

In this part . . .

- ✔ Finding a great practice space.
- ✔ Making time for the ukulele.
- ✔ Performing for an audience.
- ✔ Keeping a practice journal.
- ✔ Working on active listening.
- ✔ Go to `http://www.dummies.com/go/ukulele exercises` for ukulele audio tracks.

Chapter 15

Ten Ways to Improve Your Practice Times

In This Chapter

▶ Becoming a better ukulele player while practising less

▶ Thinking about new ways to approach practice

*B*elieve it or not, you don't need to spend hours each day practising to see gains and developments in your ukulele playing. Rather than thinking about practising more, think about practising *better*. In this chapter, I suggest to you a few different ways you can make your practice times more productive, without practising for hours and hours each day. I also give you some new ideas for approaching practice and advancing as a ukulele player.

Setting a Location

Make your practice more focused and inspired by dedicating a specific place to practise your ukulele. This could be a park, your front porch, the beach or a music 'studio' space you create in your home. The main goal is either to find a place where you completely eliminate distractions so you can focus, or to surround yourself with distractions that inspire and propel your musical creativity.

The biggest benefit to a dedicated practice space is that it allows you to unplug from the world around you. This can make you look forward to your practice times more, as they can be times of rest and peace. At the same time, your practice location can change. Don't be afraid to test a variety of locations to see what works best for you.

Scheduling a Time

Let's face it: life is busy. It's nearly impossible to find an hour to practise, or sometimes even a few minutes. For myself, I like to believe that I love the ukulele so much that I can just naturally pick it up in a moment of downtime throughout my day, but before I know it, life happens and days go by without playing. In my experience, when I've grown most as a musician, it's when I'm intentionally blocking out time in my day to practise.

The nice thing about the ukulele is that it's quite small and portable. Instead of leaving your ukulele at home, take it with you. If you're at school, bring it along and impress your friends at lunch. At work, on your break, strum out a couple songs just to get your fingers moving. If you're busy taking care of your kids, have a time in the day where you learn and practise ukulele together. Practising the ukulele doesn't have to be intense in order for it to be beneficial to your improvement as a musician.

Creating Time Limits

As I've mentioned, how long you practise isn't nearly as important as how well you practise. You don't have to practise an hour each day to become a better ukulele player (although it certainly helps). Ten to fifteen minutes of practice is better than never picking up the ukulele throughout your day. The beauty of setting a time to practise is that you know when you are going to start and end. This definitive start and end time can act as a motivator to practise as much as you can in the time you've allotted for yourself. It leaves less time for wandering.

Keeping a Practice Journal

Sitting down to practise and having no idea what to practise is very discouraging. Fortunately, this book has hundreds of exercises that you can always revisit and brush up on at any time. At the same time, though, where do you start and how and when do you know what techniques and exercises to revisit?

These questions have a way of answering themselves as you keep a practice journal. If you are writing out the things you wish to improve (that is, your goals), you're sure to spend time working on the things that help you meet those goals. For more specifics on keeping a practice journal, be sure to check out Chapter 1.

Trying Out Different Musical Styles

As a fun challenge, take a song you've heard on the radio and try to play a version of it on the ukulele. This could be a pop, country or alternative song; if you're feeling really inspired, try coming up with a version of a hip hop, dubstep or electronic song on the ukulele. The sky is the limit. The whole idea is to try to learn a song outside of a style of music that you would normally want to play on the ukulele.

To find the chords of a song you've heard, search the internet for '*song name* ukulele chords' or '*song name* guitar chords'. Often, there are more guitar chord charts for songs than ukulele chord charts. The chords of a song work the same for ukulele or guitar, although they would be played differently on each instrument.

Practising with Other People

One of the best ways to motivate yourself as a musician is by surrounding yourself with other musicians. Try to find a friend that plays ukulele. You could learn a few songs together and even play them for other people. Chances are you would have a few tips to show each other as well. This is a great way to receive encouragement and build confidence.

If you don't know anyone who plays ukulele, you have a few options. One, you can search your local area for ukulele clubs that meet and practise. You might put in some calls to different music teachers around town to see if they know of anything like that. If you can't find one, start one, or you can even join a band that might be looking for a ukulele player!

Writing a Song

Next time you practise, try writing your own song. If you've never done anything like this, to start off, choose two or three chords to create a chord progression and come up with some words and a melody. It doesn't have to be fancy, but you never know – you might just surprise yourself. By writing music, it's quite common to 'accidentally' tap into new ways of getting different sounds and tones out of the ukulele, whether through the arrangement of a simple chord progression, fingerpicking a crazy pattern that you didn't think existed, or by strumming in a way that really adds a lot of emotion.

When writing music, forget about anything and everything I've ever told you in this book or anything that anyone else has ever told you about how music should and shouldn't be. I'm serious! The writing process should be one of creativity and trying things that might not make much sense. You never know what you'll discover in the process.

If you haven't written a lot of music, chances are the first several songs you write won't be the best sounding things you've ever heard. This is okay. Don't feel like you need to write an award-winning piece of music. Writing is more about the process than the outcome. Like anything else, you only become a better songwriter with practice.

Working on Active Listening

One of the most underrated practice exercises is actively listening to music. When you practise *active listening*, you focus only on listening to a song and nothing else. There are a few specific things you can listen for:

- ✔ **The count of the song.** For example, as you count out loud and tap your toe to a song, does it make sense to count along to four, three or six? These are the most common ways to count a song. By listening to the count, you learn and further develop your understanding of rhythm in the context of actual songs.

- ✔ **The tonality of the song.** Does the overall sound of the song sound dark and complex or is it light and happy sounding? Asking this question can indicate whether the song is written in a major or minor key, since major keys tend to sound happier than minor keys.

- ✔ **The dynamics of the song.** How do the instruments in the song layer together to create energy, intensity and emotion in the overall performance? For example, in a lot of songs you hear on the radio, choruses tend to be louder in volume than verses. Noticing these dynamic changes throughout a song can direct you in how you communicate the dynamics of a song you play on the ukulele.

When practicing active listening, try to listen on a nice sounding stereo system or pair of headphones. Avoid using your phone or laptop speakers to listen to songs, since the frequency range is much narrower (in other words, you lose a lot of bass). Listening on a full-sounding sound system allows you to more easily hear the different instruments and tones that exist within the song.

Leaving Your Ukulele Out On a Stand

Part of finding the motivation to practise involves removing the barriers that stand between you and picking up the ukulele. I'm ashamed to say that I've caught myself more than once saying, 'Ah, I don't want to practise because my ukulele is buried in a case in the other room.' Pretty embarrassing, but as stupid as it is, I've found that if I eliminate this barrier, I'm more likely to pick up the ukulele and practise. This is why I always have a ukulele sitting out on a stand in my office that I can easily pick up and play.

For you, think about the things standing in the way of you practising ukulele (work, kids, school, sports, and so on) and try to find simple ways to eliminate some of the steps required to practise. For me, it was something as simple as making sure I had a ukulele on a stand within arm's length to pick up and play at any time.

Taking a Break

When it comes to learning and improving your skills, like most things, you have to give yourself time for all that learning to soak in. If you've practised something over and over and still aren't getting it, it can feel defeating, like you've hit a wall. When you find yourself getting to those points, either move on to practise something else, or take a break.

As much as ukulele is a physical activity, it's also quite mental. When you've practised for a long period of time, or spent a lot of time practising only one thing, you need to give your brain some time to recover and soak in what you just learned. Most of the time, the next time you pick up the ukulele to practise, you find that the wall you hit in your previous practice session is getting easier to climb.

Chapter 16

Ten Tips for Every Performing Ukulele Player

. . . .

In This Chapter

▶ Preparing to play the ukulele for an audience

▶ Overcoming nervousness and developing confidence

. . . .

Music is meant to be shared with others. Chances are you decided to learn how to play ukulele because you heard, saw, or knew someone who played the ukulele. It inspired something in you. For me, I learned how to play the ukulele because of my grandfather. In the same way, you have the ability, from all of your hard work and practice, to take your ukulele skills and share the joy of this small, contagious instrument with other people.

Perhaps you have dreams of playing the ukulele for thousands of people, or maybe you just want to be able to play the ukulele for a small group of friends and family. Whatever your goals are, in this chapter you can build confidence, overcome your fears and nervousness and learn how to play the ukulele for any kind of audience.

Becoming a Better Performer

Whenever a group of people gather to listen to you play a song on the ukulele, you become a performer – whether you like it or not! Depending on your personality and confidence level, playing ukulele for an audience can be one of the most intimidating things you ever do.

The funny thing about performing is that, in order to conquer the fear, anxiety and nervousness that surrounds performing, you need the experience of playing music for an audience. In other words, to become a better performer, you need to perform. Every time you play for people you acquire new skills, learn more about yourself and most importantly, build confidence. In this way, if you are shy or don't naturally like being the centre of attention, you have to be willing to take a risk and put yourself out there.

In your regular practice times, ensure that you're working on memorising a couple of classic ukulele songs, so when you're put on the spot and somebody wants you to serenade them with your lovely ukulele playing, you're ready. For starters, I recommend learning some of the classics like 'I've Been Working On the Railroad' (Chapter 4), 'Oh My Darling, Clementine' (Chapter 4) and 'Hello Ma Baby' (Chapter 5), and build your repertoire from there.

Getting Involved in the Local Music Scene

Strengthen your stage presence before an audience by watching how other musicians perform. Seek out different ukulele players and other musicians in your local area as they play music around town. As you watch, take time to ask some questions to yourself. For one, what sorts of things does the performer say from stage in between songs? What's their posture like? Do you feel like they are acknowledging you? Are you getting eye contact from them? How do they handle themselves when they make a mistake?

To all these things, notice your reaction, whether negative or positive. There will be things you like and don't like about their performance. If you can identify these things, you can learn from them and incorporate the aspects of the performance you like for the next time you make music for an audience.

As you go and hear different musicians perform, after the show, don't be afraid to introduce yourself and ask questions about their music. This can give you a lot of insight and encouragement, and you might make a new friend!

Finding a Place to Perform

Perhaps you want to get out and play your ukulele for other people but don't really know where to do that. For one, playing the ukulele is always more enjoyable when you're doing so with other people. Look around your area to see if there are any ukulele or folk music groups that meet. Often these groups have locations they perform at on a regular basis. Not only does this give you experience performing in front of an audience, but it also allows you to learn from other ukulele players and musicians. If you can't find a group like this, find a few friends and start one!

One of the best environments to practise playing the ukulele in front of an audience is at 'open mic nights' at local coffee shops, bars, pubs and restaurants. These events are a great low pressure setting to practise performing your music and meeting other musicians.

In addition, call up nursing homes, retirement communities and hospitals in your area to ask if there are any opportunities to play ukulele during an activity time. Unfortunately, more often than not, people in these settings don't get a lot of visitors, so this is a great way to brighten somebody's day in a low pressure setting. Also, check out community centres and after school programmes in your area to see whether they invite in musical entertainment.

If you write music on the ukulele and consider yourself as a singer/songwriter, it's absolutely crucial for you to get out and network with other musicians in the area, if you want to promote your music and get more fans. Go to different shows and support local musicians in your area. Musicians and artists notice you when you come to their shows and the people who run those venues also notice you. If you're a genuinely nice person, these relationships often lead to shows and opportunities to share your music with a larger audience in the future.

Building a Set List of Songs

A *set list* is a collection of songs you select to play for your audience. When it comes time to perform, it's a good idea to go into the show knowing which songs you are going to play. This ensures you play songs you've adequately practised and it prevents the sometimes overwhelming feeling of having to decide which songs to play on the spot. By being intentional about the songs you play, you create an enjoyable and memorable experience for your audience.

Building a great set list relies on a few factors. For one, people love listening to songs they know and already like. Always think about your audience. For example, would your audience gravitate more towards modern pop songs or older, classic songs? Asking questions like this can get you into the mind of your listener, which enables you to play a song they would really enjoy listening to!

Additionally, be mindful of the overall flow and dynamics between each song in your set list. For example, if you play all slow, sad songs, you most likely will put your audience to sleep, and likewise, if you play all up-tempo songs, they begin to blend together and sound the same. Try to play a good mix of songs that differ in tempo, rhythm and tone.

Preparing to Play Before an Audience

A smooth and comfortable performance starts with practice. In your practice sessions, it's a good idea to play through your set list as you would for a performance. As you play, visualise yourself playing for a crowd of people. Some find it beneficial to do a 'dress rehearsal' for a couple of close friends.

At the same time, there's only so much you can prepare for when it comes to playing ukulele for a group of people. In that setting, you start to feel nerves, excitement and stress that isn't normally experienced during your solitude times of practice. This is why it's so important to get out there and just start playing. The first step is the hardest, but it gets easier.

If you tend to be a shy or more reserved person, don't be afraid to take a risk and put yourself out there. You're probably more ready and equipped than you give yourself credit. On the other hand, if you like being the centre of attention, ensure you're putting in adequate practice time so you can provide a good performance for your audience.

Handling Nerves Right Before the Show

It's the big moment. It's about fifteen minutes before going out on stage. Butterflies are swarming your stomach, your heart is racing and your body starts to ache from tension. You start to grow frustrated with yourself because you're asking, 'Why in the world am I so nervous? I hate this feeling!'

Typically, when it comes to performing, we tend to think of nervousness, anxiousness and those pre-show jitters as a bad thing. At times, it can be crippling, even if you're only playing for a few people, but if you use these nervous feelings in the right way, you can actually help your performance.

In 1908, psychologists Robert Yerkes and John Dodson developed the Yerkes-Dodson law which states that performance increases, whether that be physical or mental performance, with a certain amount of arousal, such as through stress, anxiety and nerves, but if the level of arousal is too high, performance decreases. In other words, a certain amount of nervousness and anxiousness can motivate you to play ukulele well, but if you let the nervousness get the best of you, you can feel overwhelmed, and overthink your performance to the point where you make a lot of mistakes.

To find the right balance between being excited and not being controlled by nerves, try a couple things before the next time you perform. First, starting a half hour before the show, practise some breathing exercises (see Chapter 2). Allowing more oxygen into your body has a relaxing affect and can help lower your heart rate, which combats a feeling of anxiousness.

Often times when nervousness seizes your body, muscles start to tense up, so as you practise breathing, stretch out your arms, shoulders and neck to keep tension at bay. Lastly, depending on if you are an extroverted or introverted personality, surround yourself with other people to distract yourself from being nervous and get you pumped up, or find a quiet place to think, pray, or meditate.

Mastering the Art of Focus

Now, it's time to take the stage. During the performance, you want to be as focused as possible on the songs you are playing (that is, you don't want to be thinking about you're going to eat for dinner afterwards!).

Part of being focused is trusting yourself. Before playing for an audience, you should have played through your set list dozens of times in practice. By the time of the performance, your hands and fingers are very familiar with how to play the songs. Don't let your mind get the best of you. Let your hands and fingers do their work.

Before playing a song, gather and collect yourself before you strum the strings. If you've ever watched classically trained musicians perform, they often pause before they begin a song to clear their minds, ensure their breathing is under control, and to think about the very first note.

As you play through a song, avoid negative thinking. For example, if you're coming up on a tricky chord or passage, don't think, 'I hope I don't mess this part up,' because chances are you will overthink it and mess up. If you do make a mistake, it's okay. No sweat! Just continue to smile and keep playing.

Remembering to Breathe

Whatever you do, don't hold your breath while you're performing. Stay loose and remember to breathe. Unfortunately, I learned this lesson the hard way.

While performing during my first guitar recital at university, I forgot to breathe. It wasn't good. The songs were quite easy, so much so that I could play them with my eyes closed, but when it came time to sit in that room and play them for an audience with all eyes on me, I forgot the most simple task of all: breathing. Before I knew it, my hands were shaking, sweat was dripping from my forehead, and I started forgetting entire measures of music.

It was a strange experience and very discouraging. The lesson learned is that not only does breathing help calm your nerves before a performance, but it also helps you stay relaxed and calm during a performance. After this experience, as I perform now, I always remember to take a couple good deep breaths before I start into a song.

Engaging With Your Audience

Even if you make a gazillion mistakes and mess up, your audience tends to forget those if they feel like they were able to engage with you as a person. As you're performing, remember to smile, look at your audience and even laugh. Avoid looking down or closing your eyes. In some cases, you might close your eyes to communicate a certain level of emotion, but by looking at your audience, you make them feel apart of your performance.

Just relax. If you look like you're having fun, your audience will have fun and feel comfortable. Part of performing is having a humility about yourself on stage. Don't take yourself so seriously.

Don't feel pressure to always have to say something before or after you play a song. For familiar songs, ask your audience to sing along. Sometimes it's enough to tell your audience the title of the song and that you hope they enjoy it. If you do decide to talk, you might tell them a story or a memory you have with the song. Keep it short to keep your audience's attention. Lastly, don't forget to warmly thank your audience for giving you their attention and listening.

Being Confident in Yourself

Developing confidence in yourself as a performer requires time, experience and practice. Within this, there is a lot of messing up, and at times, a feeling of complete failure. Embrace these mistakes, and in those moments you feel like you really mess up a song, take a moment to laugh at yourself. Just come back to that song the next time you practise.

A lot of times people admire you for getting up in front of an audience to play music. Even if you're a shy person, be encouraged because some of the most famous musicians and performers in the last century were known for being shy – people like Bob Dylan, Michael Jackson, Elvis Presley and Ella Fitzgerald.

Most importantly, you have to understand that you have the ability to bring joy to someone's life through your ukulele playing. This is the nature of music. Whether you would like to think so or not, there are unique qualities about your demeanour, voice and playing that cannot be matched by anyone else. This is what makes someone so enjoyable and memorable to listen to. You don't have to be better than someone else to share the joy of ukulele with another person – an honest performance that is true to yourself is all it takes!

About the Author

Brett McQueen is a lifelong ukulele player, performer and writer. He learned to play the ukulele at the age of six from his grandfather, who taught him to play the classic folk song 'I've Been Working On the Railroad'. In 2010, Brett took his enduring enthusiasm for ukulele forward to establish www.UkuleleTricks.com, which has become one of the most widely recognised ukulele lesson websites on the internet, passing over six million views since its inception. Over 3,000 students and counting are enrolled in his online ukulele lesson course at www.UkuleleTricks.com. He is the author of the digital ukulele lesson book *Your First Ukulele Lesson and Then Some*, which has been read and used by over 30,000 people, from kids as young as 6 years old to adults as old as 92 years old, to learn how to play the ukulele.

As you read this book, if you have any questions or comments about playing the ukulele, contact Brett at brett@ukuleletricks.com.

Alistair Wood, Contributing Editor to this book, is a ukulele enthusiast, arranger, and writer, and the author of *Ukulele For Dummies*. He first picked up a ukulele at the age of 16 and spent five years working out which way round the strings were supposed to go. Once that hurdle was leapt, he quickly became a devotee and launched the website UkuleleHunt.com in 2007.

Since then, UkuleleHunt.com has gone on to be the most popular ukulele blog on the Net, attracting over 6 million views and becoming the online hub of the ukulele scene. His expertise on the current ukulele boom has lead to his opinions being sought by *The Guardian, The New York Times,* and BBC News.

You can contact Alistair at ukulelehunt@gmail.com.

Dedication

From Brett: For my grandfather, Jerry McQueen, who taught and inspired me to play the ukulele.

Author's Acknowledgments

I am grateful to Mike Baker, Simon Bell, Ben Kemble and the rest of the talented team at Wiley for all of their hard work and dedication to this book. Special thanks to Alistair Wood, from www.UkuleleHunt.com and author of *Ukulele For Dummies*, who recommended me to author this book and for his feedback during the writing process. His input into this book was brilliant and pivotal.

I'd also like to thank Nolan Rossi at RF Studios who recorded, mixed, and mastered the audio examples for this book. Thank you for easing my mind in the studio and challenging me in darts – I'll be practising for next time.

The biggest and most affectionate thanks to my mom, dad, and brother Ian for always supporting me. Grandpa McQueen, thank you for giving me the gift of music; it's impacted my life in a remarkable way. Thank you to my family, friends, and housemates who have tolerated me with patience for the past several months and have encouraged me as I've been working on this project. I love you all.

Last, but certainly not least, I extend the deepest thanks to my students, friends, and readers at www.UkuleleTricks.com. Our conversations through email and comments have been such an overwhelming encouragement and motivation as I've written this book. Thank you for supporting me and allowing me to pursue music through the ukulele.

Publisher's Acknowledgments

We're proud of this book; please send us your comments at http://dummies.custhelp.com. For other comments, please contact our Customer Care Department within the U.S. at 877-762-2974, outside the U.S. at (001) 317-572-3993, or fax 317-572-4002.

Some of the people who helped bring this book to market include the following:

Acquisitions, Editorial, and Vertical Websites

Project Editor: Simon Bell

Commissioning Editor: Mike Baker

Assistant Editor: Ben Kemble

Development Editor: Simon Bell

Copy Editor: Kate O'Leary

Contributing Editor: Al Wood

Proofreader: Mary White

Production Manager: Daniel Mersey

Publisher: Miles Kendall

Vertical Websites: Rich Graves

Cover Photos: © Pechjira Lueprasert / iStockphoto

Composition Services

Project Coordinator: Kristie Rees

Layout and Graphics: Carrie A. Cesavice, Jennifer Creasey, Joyce Haughey, Christin Swinford

FOR DUMMIES®

Making Everything Easier!™

BUSINESS

Bookkeeping
FOR
DUMMIES

978-1-118-34689-1

Pop Up Business
FOR
DUMMIES

978-1-118-44349-1

Starting & Running a Business
ALL-IN-ONE
FOR
DUMMIES

978-1-119-97527-4

MUSIC

Mandolin
FOR
DUMMIES

978-1-119-94276-4

Ukulele
FOR
DUMMIES

978-0-470-97799-6

DJing
FOR
DUMMIES

978-0-470-66372-1

HOBBIES

Stargazing
FOR
DUMMIES

978-1-118-41156-8

Keeping Chickens
FOR
DUMMIES

978-1-119-99417-6

Beekeeping
FOR
DUMMIES

978-1-119-97250-1

Asperger's Syndrome For Dummies
978-0-470-66087-4

Basic Maths For Dummies
978-1-119-97452-9

Body Language For Dummies, 2nd Edition
978-1-119-95351-7

Boosting Self-Esteem For Dummies
978-0-470-74193-1

Business Continuity For Dummies
978-1-118-32683-1

Cricket For Dummies
978-0-470-03454-5

Diabetes For Dummies, 3rd Edition
978-0-470-97711-8

eBay For Dummies, 3rd Edition
978-1-119-94122-4

English Grammar For Dummies
978-0-470-05752-0

Flirting For Dummies
978-0-470-74259-4

IBS For Dummies
978-0-470-51737-6

ITIL For Dummies
978-1-119-95013-4

Management For Dummies, 2nd Edition
978-0-470-97769-9

Managing Anxiety with CBT For Dummies
978-1-118-36606-6

Neuro-linguistic Programming For Dummies, 2nd Edition
978-0-470-66543-5

Nutrition For Dummies, 2nd Edition
978-0-470-97276-2

Organic Gardening For Dummies
978-1-119-97706-3

FOR DUMMIES®

Making Everything Easier! ™

SELF-HELP

Cognitive Behavioural Therapy For Dummies, 2nd Edition
Rhena Branch
Rob Willson
978-0-470-66541-1

Creative Visualization For Dummies
Robin Nixon
978-1-119-99264-6

Mindfulness For Dummies
Shamash Alidina
978-0-470-66086-7

LANGUAGES

Spanish For Dummies
Pedro Vázquez Bermejo
Susana Wald
978-0-470-68815-1

Polish For Dummies
Daria Gabryanczyk
978-1-119-97959-3

British Sign Language For Dummies
city Lit
978-0-470-69477-0

HISTORY

The Tudors For Dummies
David Loades
Mei Trow
978-0-470-68792-5

Medieval History For Dummies
Stephen Batchelor
978-0-470-74783-4

British History For Dummies, 3rd Edition
Dr. Seán Lang
978-0-470-97819-1

Origami Kit For Dummies
978-0-470-75857-1

Overcoming Depression For Dummies
978-0-470-69430-5

Positive Psychology For Dummies
978-0-470-72136-0

PRINCE2 For Dummies, 2009 Edition
978-0-470-71025-8

Project Management For Dummies
978-0-470-71119-4

Psychology Statistics For Dummies
978-1-119-95287-9

Psychometric Tests For Dummies
978-0-470-75366-8

Renting Out Your Property For Dummies, 3rd Edition
978-1-119-97640-0

Rugby Union For Dummies, 3rd Edition
978-1-119-99092-5

Sage One For Dummies
978-1-119-95236-7

Self-Hypnosis For Dummies
978-0-470-66073-7

Storing and Preserving Garden Produce For Dummies
978-1-119-95156-8

Teaching English as a Foreign Language For Dummies
978-0-470-74576-2

Time Management For Dummies
978-0-470-77765-7

Training Your Brain For Dummies
978-0-470-97449-0

Voice and Speaking Skills For Dummies
978-1-119-94512-3

Work-Life Balance For Dummies
978-0-470-71380-8

FOR DUMMIES®

Making Everything Easier! ™

COMPUTER BASICS

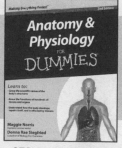

978-1-118-11533-6

978-0-470-61454-9

978-0-470-49743-2

DIGITAL PHOTOGRAPHY

978-1-118-09203-3

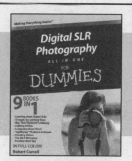

978-0-470-76878-5

978-1-118-00472-2

SCIENCE AND MATHS

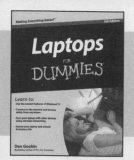

978-0-470-92326-9

978-0-470-55964-2

978-0-470-90324-7

Art For Dummies
978-0-7645-5104-8

Computers For Seniors For Dummies, 3rd Edition
978-1-118-11553-4

Criminology For Dummies
978-0-470-39696-4

Currency Trading For Dummies, 2nd Edition
978-0-470-01851-4

Drawing For Dummies, 2nd Edition
978-0-470-61842-4

Forensics For Dummies
978-0-7645-5580-0

French For Dummies, 2nd Edition
978-1-118-00464-7

Guitar For Dummies, 2nd Edition
978-0-7645-9904-0

Hinduism For Dummies
978-0-470-87858-3

Index Investing For Dummies
978-0-470-29406-2

Islamic Finance For Dummies
978-0-470-43069-9

Knitting For Dummies, 2nd Edition
978-0-470-28747-7

Music Theory For Dummies, 2nd Edition
978-1-118-09550-8

Office 2010 For Dummies
978-0-470-48998-7

Piano For Dummies, 2nd Edition
978-0-470-49644-2

Photoshop CS6 For Dummies
978-1-118-17457-9

Schizophrenia For Dummies
978-0-470-25927-6

WordPress For Dummies, 5th Edition
978-1-118-38318-6

Think you can't learn it in a day? Think again!

The *In a Day* e-book series from *For Dummies* gives you quick and easy access to learn a new skill, brush up on a hobby, or enhance your personal or professional life — all in a day. Easy!

Available as PDF, eMobi and Kindle